Beads and Threads:

A New Technique for Fiber Jewelry

by
Diane Fitzgerald
and
Helen Banes

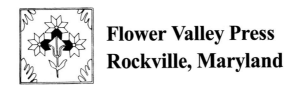

Flower Valley Press
Rockville, Maryland

Book Design by Dan Bress

Printed and bound in Hong Kong

Library of Congress Catalog Card Number: 93-71699
ISBN 0-9620543-6-4

10 9 8 7 6 5 4 3 2

Flower Valley Press
Box 645
Rockville, MD 20848

Contents

Introduction   v

Foreword   vi

Dedications   vii

Acknowledgments   ix

About the Authors   xii

Chapter 1.   A Gallery of Necklaces   1

Chapter 2.   Designing Your Own Necklace   33

Chapter 3.   Weaving Your Necklace   55

Chapter 4.   Patterns   73

Chapter 5.   Finding or Making the Perfect Beads for Your Necklace   113

Other Books and Publications   125

Bead Societies   127

Sources of Beads   128

Photo & Illustration Credits   129

Index   132

1. *Le Grande Kabyle* **by Helen Banes**

Introduction

At last! For all of us who love to hold a threaded needle and who have a special stash of beads waiting to become adornment, here is a technique that combines the best of both in the form of needlewoven jewelry. Needleweaving with beads is a technique which incorporates beads into woven jewelry: a necklace, bracelet or even a belt. The weaving is done on a simple loom made of a board and pins. After warp threads are passed around the pins and the beads slipped into place, the in and out of the weaving begins. This is simple to do and offers exciting possibilities for expressing your own creativity.

As a hobby or as an artistic expression, needleweaving is ideal: it offers a wonderful way to combine both fibers and beads in new and unusual ways. Like knitting, crochet or other forms of needlework, needleweaving is portable. Once your piece is designed and the beads are in place you can pick it up and take it with you. And lastly, it requires little initial investment. With just a board, pins and small amounts of colorful thread and beads, you can create necklaces as exciting as those you see in this book.

Weaving is a relaxing pursuit. Needleweaving projects are small, take shape quickly and demand little physical stamina or energy. Watching your work grow and develop into a unique and original creation is satisfying and rewarding. Once you have mastered the simple techniques, you'll want to try new designs and experiment with new combinations of colors and beads.

The special needlewoven jewelry techniques described in this book were developed by Helen Banes. Her simplified techniques for integrating beads and fiber are the result of several years of experimentation and many more years of teaching the methods to people across North America.

Gather your beads and your thread and get ready for a wonderful new adventure!

Foreword

The best art of each generation simultaneously joins tradition while overturning it.

Exquisite beads, amulets and artifacts have for centuries been combined with fibers to create stunning and imaginative adornments. African, Native American, Pre-Columbian, Egyptian, Chinese and East Indian cultures made extensive use of needleweaving techniques to fashion colorful, highly textured ornaments that decorate the body and transform the human spirit.

The highly refined and elegant pectoral neckpieces created by Helen Banes join a long tradition of body embellishment. Simultaneously, Banes overturns those traditions with her inventive and dynamic sense of 20th century color, pattern and design. Never a slave to her technique, Banes is a master at meshing disparate materials such as beads, artifacts, threads and coins from diverse cultures into a beautifully integrated new form of expression that transcends technique.

Helen Banes' use of fiber and beads mutually reinforce the rich qualities and possibilities inherent in these materials. Through several years of experimentation, Banes single-handedly invented a new technique which allowed her to integrate beads onto warp threads, thus creating a unified whole in contrast to the usual conventional application of beads on a textile surface.

She further integrates her woven neckpieces to the human form by fine weaving her threads so that the finished piece accommodates the subtle contours of the body. This makes an extremely comfortable and elegant form of wearable art.

Widely traveled, Helen Banes developed a curiosity about other cultures and their use of body embellishments. Her serious research into ethnic groups, period textiles, their symbols and craft methods has given her needleworked neckpieces a richness and vibrant visual resonance that echoes across centuries.

Please join the authors as they lead you on an adventurous and passionate journey steeped in the rich traditions of history, design, technique and symbolism as reflected in the body adornments of many cultures. By making a fiber and bead neckpiece as suggested in this publication, you will be joining a tradition thousands of years old. If you remain receptive to the infinite possibilities you may overturn those traditions by creating a new and exciting form of needlewoven jewelry that will enrich our cultural and visual heritage.

> \- Michael W. Monroe
> Curator-in-Charge
> Renwick Gallery, National Museum of American Art
> Smithsonian Institution, Washington, DC.

Dedication

To my mother, who taught me to hold a needle,

To my father, who taught me to love books,

and

To my husband, who taught me to use a computer.

—We stand on the shoulders of giants...

- Diane Fitzgerald

2. Diane Fitzgerald.

Dedication

3. Helen Banes.

To The Generations of Creative Women in my Family:

My great-grandmother Freyda, a self-taught fiber artist in White Russia who decorated peasant skirts and blouses with naturally dyed yarns.

My grandmother Tybee, who created an unlimited supply of hand-crocheted sweaters for each of her many grandchildren.

My mother Ida, of blessed memory, who encouraged me to practice. Her active hands were always knitting or sewing. Her brilliant mind remembered every song or book she read. Her first novel was published at the age of seventy-five.

My devoted sister Leonore, a serious artist of ceramics and painting who has had the patience to watch over me.

My daughters, Susan, Ruby and Sally, each creating new directions in scholarship and the arts.

My granddaughters Mimi and Amy, who are determined to carry on the traditions.

- Helen Richter Banes

Acknowledgments

The following people deserve generous thanks for their assistance in bringing this book to its tangible form: Barb Hjort who invited me to attend the class taught by Helen Banes in 1988, where it all started for me; each student who has taken my class and helped me learn to express the ideas in so many different ways; the Department of Design, Housing and Apparel of the University of Minnesota where I learned the language and structure of design, without which this book could not have been written; to Jana Burnham who helped me get started in the bead business; to my husband, Alan Shilepsky, who staked my bead inventory so that I could open my shop, Beautiful Beads, and who is my understanding and loyal companion; to my friends in the Upper Midwest Bead Society who share my fun and love of beads; to the members of Surface Design Minnesota who never fail to inspire me when I am with them; to all the bead artists who contributed slides of their work, showing the diverse directions in which this technique can evolve and finally, to Helen Banes who has given so much of herself to me and to this book.

Because I will probably never have the opportunity to meet most of you who read this book, I would like to ask you to send me a photo of you wearing a necklace you have made.

I always tell students who take my class that the tuition covers my advice and help until they complete their necklace. Although we've done our best to be careful in writing these instructions, you may come upon problems that you can't solve. If you get stuck and can't figure out what to do, please write to me at Beautiful Beads, 115 Hennepin Avenue, Minneapolis, MN 55401. Enclose a large self-addressed, stamped envelope and I will reply as soon as possible. If necessary, draw a picture to accompany your question.

- Diane Fitzgerald

Acknowledgments

After many years of assuring my fiber students that the information and illustrations about my original process would be compiled into a book, I never thought it could actually be accomplished. Even after several of my students wrote articles about my fiber jewelry in various journals: Rona Subotnik in Ornament Magazine (Vol. 5, No. 4, 1982); Doris Hendershot in The Flying Needle (February, 1987); Susan Beaudry in Threads Magazine (February, 1990); and Diane Fitzgerald in Ornament Magazine (Summer, 1991), I still could not figure out a way to add another project to my complicated schedule.

Being a founding member of the Fiberworks Gallery in the Torpedo Factory Art Center in historic Old Town of Alexandria, Virginia meant participating every week, while creating new works to be exhibited each month. I could not relinquish the opportunity to meet the thousands of appreciative visitors to our gallery, or to lose the companionship and stimulation of the past and present members after seventeen years of their support and encouragement.

How could I refuse the many requests to teach workshops to the enthusiastic students who kept challenging me to extend my repertoire, since many of these advanced students have continued to meet regularly for at least fifteen years?

When energetic Diane Fitzgerald insisted that we could complete this book in spite of the distance between our homes and the traveling times taken by our teaching schedules, I was delighted at the prospect and agreed to the project.

All of my teachers have influenced me, but none in so many ways as my husband, Daniel, who has been for more than fifty years, my best friend, travel companion, financial supporter and gentle critic. At every opportunity, I thank him for bringing our family to the Washington, D.C. area which has provided the opportunity to explore and then to teach at the Smithsonian Museums and the Textile Museum.

He invited me to accompany him on his world-wide travels where we shared the adventure of discovering treasures of artifacts and the pleasure of new associations. He influenced me to appreciate Mozart, Shakespeare and the mysticism of Kabbalah.

Other teachers led to unexpected paths. Frances Allis, my first modern dance teacher in Chicago, taught me that the body is the most expressive instrument to be used in innovative creation. Ben Abramowitz, a painting teacher at the Graduate School of the Department of Agriculture, encouraged me to paint with the freedom of an abstract expressionist. The late Sidney Gross, a well-known New York-trained artist, who was my teacher for four years at the graduate art department at the University of Maryland, and whose understanding of applied color theory and applied psychology gave me the confidence to continue painting. Ron Goodman, my first teacher of fiber arts at the Smithsonian Institution Resident Associates program, opened a new direction for my urge to explore another medium. After twenty years of continuing contact, I consider him an outstanding teacher and a good friend.

I would need to write another book to list all the persons who have influenced my work and have encouraged me to write this book. Our publisher, Seymour Bress, appreciated the problem of fiber artists having their books properly designed and published. He has the courage to support our art and to make the book available to our past and future students.

- Helen Banes

About the authors . . .

Diane Fitzgerald lives in Minneapolis, Minnesota. She is happiest when she has a bowl of beads and a threaded needle to create with...

"It all started at the age of five with a simple dish towel. To keep me amused, my mother gave me a dish towel to embroider while she braided my hair. The familiar Walco bead loom came next and I worked with that until my beads were gone. As an adult, I worked in needlepoint and then did quilting, but neither were as enticing as beads which are transparent, reflective and three-dimensional. I had always collected beads but hadn't experimented with them until I took Helen Banes' class at the Textile Arts Centre in Chicago. That class changed my life. When I couldn't find the variety of beads I wanted, I searched out bead sources and opened my own shop, Beautiful Beads. Soon after, I began teaching classes in a variety of bead assemblage techniques, including needlewoven necklaces. A B.A. in Journalism, M.A. in Mass Communication and courses in color and design at the University of Minnesota gave me the background and vocabulary necessary to teach and write about beads, beadwork and fiberarts."

Helen Banes traces the roots of her fascination with pattern and body art to her early childhood training as a modern dancer in Chicago in the 1920s. She went on to study dance and education at the University of Illinois. After marrying, settling in the Washington, D.C. area, and raising a family, she began graduate work in art, studying painting and color theory with Sidney Gross at the University of Maryland in the mid-1960s. A course in weaving with Ron Goodman in 1969 led to her earliest experiments in fiber art. From the start, she used off-loom techniques and bold colors in surprising combinations to create a sense of motion. "To me the loom seemed limiting. One got caught in a solid woven surface. My own approach was to look at the process like a painting, working on a piece from all directions. When I painted, I almost never used an easel. Inspired by Jackson Pollock, I spread the canvas on the floor and danced around it." Traveling with her husband, a consultant for the World Health Organization, to Europe, the Middle East, Central and South America and Asia, Helen began collecting and studying ancient beads and folk textiles. These sparked design ideas for her own work, as did classes in both Western and non-Western fiber techniques. Her desire to incorporate beads and other artifacts into her woven pieces and her interest in wearable art that could move with the body led to her most important innovation–the method of stringing beads on a double warp, using a shaped loom on a lightweight portable board. Helen Banes is a founding member of the Fiber Workshop, located in the Torpedo Factory in Alexandria, Virginia, and also of the Bead Society of Greater Washington.

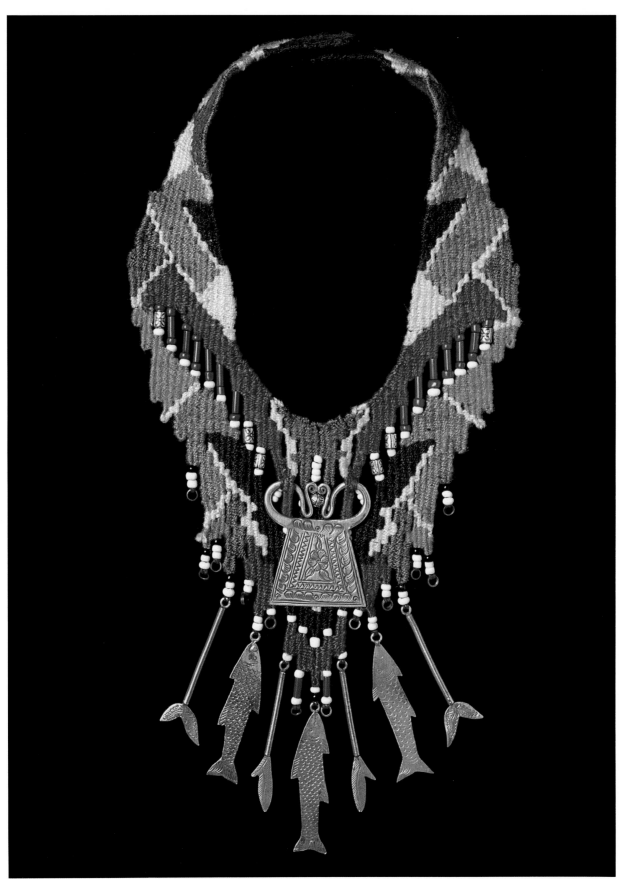

4. *Spirit Lock of Thailand* by Helen Banes.

A Gallery of Necklaces

This chapter will show you the exciting range of artistry that has resulted from Helen Banes' technique. Both Helen's work, and that of her students are shown on the following pages, along with comments about the technique and the pieces. We begin with Helen's work.

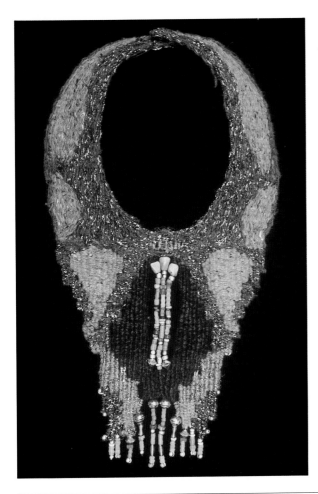

5. *Homage to Maria Martinez* **by Helen Banes. Design inspired by the pottery of the San Ildefonso potter, Maria Martinez. The clay and Navaho silver beads relate to the Southwest Native American crafts.**

I am often asked how I can bear to part with my necklaces when they have taken so much of my time. In response, my colleague, B.J. Adams, gave me this advice: "All you need is a good color photograph or slide so that you can refer to it when you want to recall the design or to use it for teaching purposes." I have taken her advice, and I also take a color photocopy of each piece, so that I have an exact copy of the scale and colors of the necklace. A photocopy will reproduce even the details of the beads.

- Helen Banes

HELEN BANES

Necklaces with African Motifs

6. *Timbuktu*. **(top left) Its brilliant colors were inspired by African tribal textiles.**

7. *Fetish Adornment*. **(top right) Inspired by a small wooden fetish figure believed to repel any malevolent influences; exhibited in the Michael Rockefeller Wing of the Metropolitan Museum of Art, New York City.**

8. *Asante Gold*. **(left) Gold washed beads made by the Asante people of Ivory Coast using the lost wax method.**

Necklaces with Pre-Columbian Motifs

9. *Tairona Pectoral.* (top left) Removable gold pin in an anthropomorphic design. Collection of Mr. and Mrs. Clarence Goldberg.

10. *Peruvian Pectoral with Coins.* (top right) Hand-painted ceramic beads from Peru.

11. *Tolima Figure.* (left) A replica of a Pre-Columbian gold figure with three green stones, which are ancient Peruvian adornments.

12. *Mask of Xipe-Totec.* (top left) This ingenious necklace can be disassembled into three parts: a pin, a small pendant necklace, and a larger pendant. The pin is Mexican gilded silver and the feather-like head piece and jade-like earspools are made of polymer clay.

13. *Mask of Xipe-Totec.* (top right) The elements of the necklace, separated.

14. *Brazilian Tribal.* (left) Inspired by a tribal comb made of raffia woven on wooden thorns. Necklace woven in twill weave pattern with dangles of ostrich egg shell.

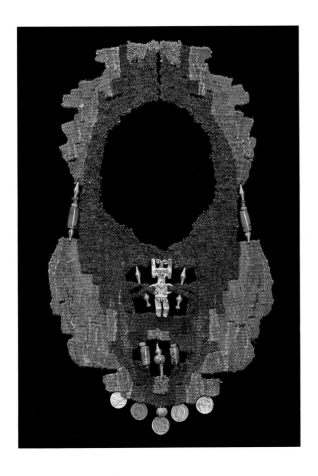

15. *Colombian Gold.* (top left) Metal fetish figure from Colombia with gold-colored coins.

Necklace with a Chinese Motif

16. *Chinese Cloud Collar.* (top right) Exhibited at the Renwick Gallery, Washington, D.C. and in the Smithsonian Traveling Exhibition, "Good as Gold: Alternative Materials in American Jewelry (1981)."

Necklace with an Egyptian Motif

17. *Royal Pectoral with Scarab* (left)

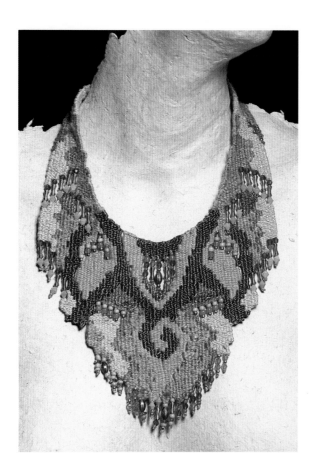

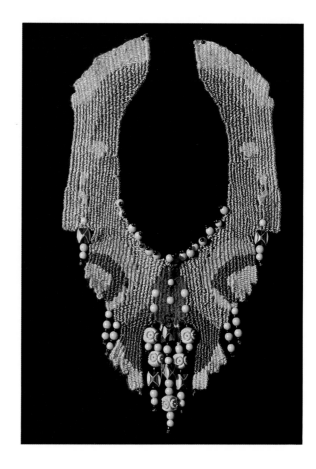

Necklaces Based on Art Deco Motifs and Designs

18. *Clarisse's Collar.* (top left) Inspired by the design and colors of an earthenware vase created by Clarisse Cliff, a 1920's English potter. From the collections of Adeline Mazur and Patricia Kauffmann.

19. *Coral Cascade.* (top right) Beads are early plastic of the 1930's.

20. *Tiffany No. 2.* (left) Removable Mexican silver pin with amethyst stone; Czechoslovakian faceted crystal beads. With pin, collection of Mrs. Marion Richman.

21. *Urim and Thummim*. (top right) Inspired by the description of the breast plate of the high priest in Exodus Ch. 28, v. 15:

    "You shall make a breastplate of gold, blue and purple yarns and of fine twisted linens. Set in it four rows of stones. The stones shall correspond to the twelve sons of Israel...On the breastplate you shall place the Urim and Thummim, so that they are over Aaron's heart."

    The stones representing the twelve tribes of Israel are made of polymer clay. The weft thread is metallic gold; fringes and tassels are silk and rayon thread.

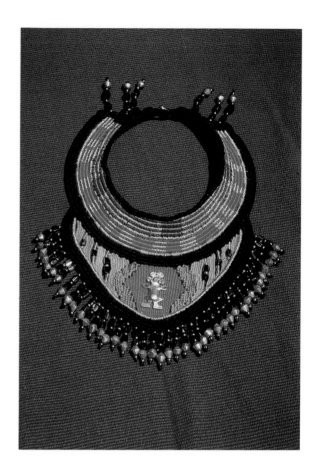

STUDENTS' WORK

22. *Scarab* **by Judy Benson. (top left) An earlier course in coiled basketry lead to this unusual combination of coiling and weaving techniques. Judy begins with a general mental image of how she wants the piece to look and a selection of colors which she adds to or subtracts from as the piece assumes form.**

23. *Frog* **by Judy Benson. (top right)**

24. *Lady Helen* **by Christofer Aven. (left) This piece was designed as part of the Christofer Collection, a series of ten medieval wedding veils modeled at the Chicago National Bridal Trade Show in 1990 and 1991. An important part of the design is the pleasing proportion of strands of beads to the overall piece. Overly long strands would distort the shape of the piece.**

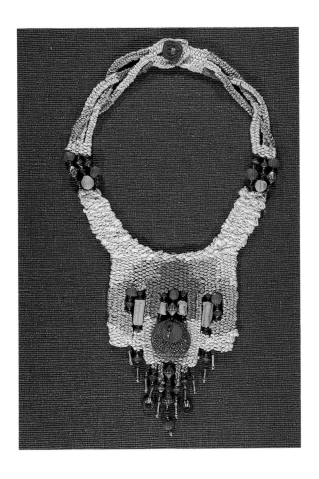

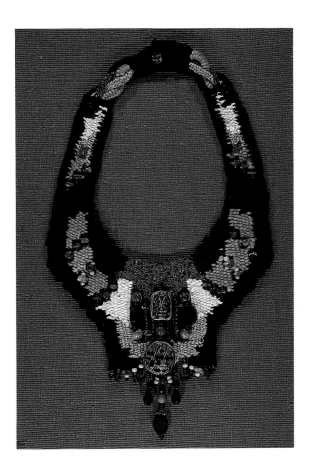

25. *First Effort* by Judy Ehrhardt. (top left) The soft, southwestern desert theme complements the Georgia red clay of the hand-built ornaments which are similar to the red rock of the Arizona landscape. Beads and major pieces are Georgia red and speckled stoneware.

26. *Aztec Night* by Judy Ehrhardt. (top right) The goldstone, black horn, and leopard-skin agate beads blend well with the glazed stoneware which Ms. Ehrhardt produces herself. The drama and power of the Aztec culture are strikingly represented by the contrasting colors of the pearl cotton.

27. *Autumn Blaze* by Kimberly Childs. (left) Inspired by the changing colors of fall, Kimberly collected leaves from a local botanic garden and matched them to threads at a stitchery shop. To augment her thread and beads, she made additional beads from polymer clay, sometimes insetting small stones into the beads for greater effect. "I enjoy the soothing movements of weaving and since this technique is portable, I take it with me everywhere. As I travel, I search for interesting beads and threads and so my work takes on the flavor of the places I have visited," she said.

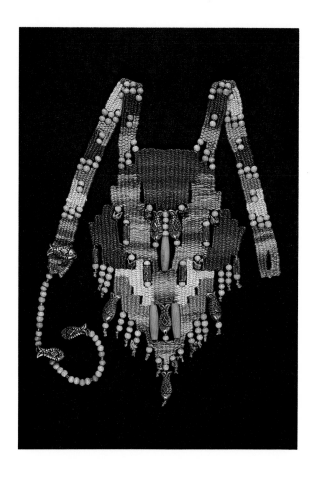

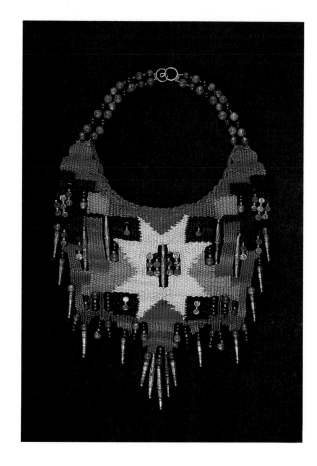

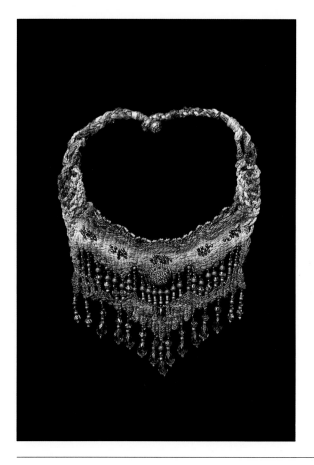

28. *Nantucket Fantasy* by Virginia E. Hird. (top left) A member of the Shore Fiber Arts Guild, Virginia exhibited three neckpieces at the Mid-Atlantic Fiber Association Conference at Bucknell University, Pennsylvania, in 1991. "The green birds, coral beads and silver fish reminded me of happy hours spent walking the beach of Cape Cod Bay and the water color cotton seemed to be part of the Cape Cod sunset," said Virginia.

29. *Andean Starburst* by Virginia E. Hird. (top right) The center star of this neckpiece was inspired by a motif in an Andean four-cornered hat. The bold star motif might also be familiar to quilters as the "Lone Star" pattern.

30. *Orpheum* by Barb Hjort. (left) "As a child it was a treat to go to the movies in the big downtown theater, the Orpheum. I was particularly enraptured by the time-worn, gold-brocade curtains. They hung everywhere: stage, boxes, balconies. I would wake at night dreaming that the fringe had been alive, that it was crawling off the walls, right towards me!" With such vivid memories, it's no wonder Barb was able to create such a luscious piece. The focal point is an antique button given to her by a great aunt.

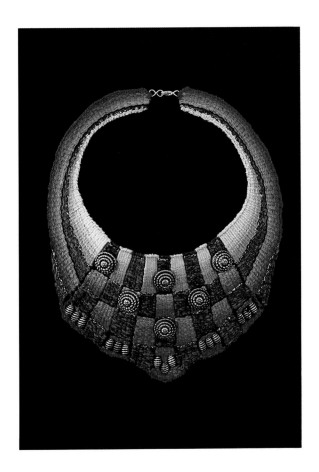

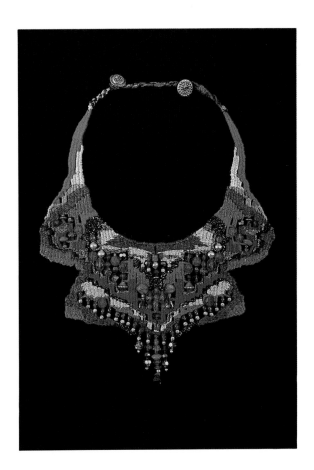

31. *Seventeen Blue* by Barb Hjort. (top left) This necklace was warped with thread in a radiating pattern and the weaving was done in a circular fashion. Seventeen shades of blue cotton and linen fibers were used.

32. *Jeweltone* by Barb Hjort. (top right) This piece was made with threads matched to those in a silk dress. Matching thread to a favorite skirt, blouse or dress gives a head start in planning a necklace.

33. *Geode* by Barb Hjort. (left) The natural shapes of geodes inspired this very successful piece. Like "Seventeen Blue" (above), this necklace was warped with thread in a radiating pattern but with an irregular outer shape. Collection of Diane Fitzgerald.

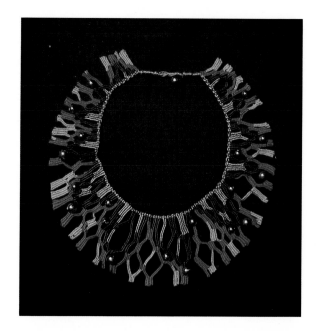

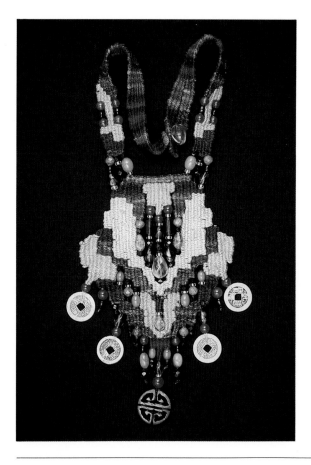

34. *Sun Dance* by Pamela Penney. (top left)

35. *Flora* by Pamela Penney. (top right) "There are two elements that I find critical to my pieces. The first important aspect of my neckpieces is what I term the 'voids.' As I weave, I deliberately distort the warp threads to create open spaces. These empty spaces are as critical to the composition as the actual weaving itself. In this way I more closely associate my needleweaving with traditional lace making techniques than to tapestry weaving. Secondly, my design process is an evolution. By this I mean that although I have an overall concept in mind and I develop an overall shape for the warp, I do not chart out or plan the weaving itself. I let the design come to me as I proceed with the weaving. I put the beads on the warp and change colors as I intuitively feel they are needed. In this way, my neckpieces are balanced from side to side but are always asymmetrical."

36. *Victorian Parlor* by Patricia K. Jeydel. (left) "This piece contains elements found in my sister's attic: Chinese coins from our grandmother's sewing basket, jet beads from great-grandmother's necklace, and various amber beads. The green glass beads and crystal rondelles had resided for years in an old box of buttons, and belonged to these same ladies."

37. *Inca Princess* by **Diane Fitzgerald. (top left)**

38. *Of Royal Blood* by **Diane Fitzgerald. (top right)**

39. *Miss Piggy* by **Diane Fitzgerald. (left)**

40. *Anasazi Bird.* by Ann Shafer. (top left)"This necklace is a representation of an Anasazi (prehistoric Indians who lived in the American Southwest — direct ancestors of the Pueblo Indians) bird, a thunderbird, common to many Indian tribes. I chose to name it "Anasazi Bird" to recognize the rich culture the Anasazi Indians left behind in this area. The silver represents Indian jewelry and the blue the fantastic blue sky. Creating necklaces is a change for me — since I usually weave and design clothing — and one which I love."

41. *Untitled No. 1* by Barbara W. Saslow. (top right) "The inspiration for my work usually starts with either a color scheme or the beads themselves. It is not uncommon for me to awaken with colors on my mind, and further ideas come to me during my daily swim. Then I study my ever-growing bead supply (Collecting beads is a disease you know!) and mail-order catalogs. My design usually begins to evolve at this point. However, it also could work in reverse! Sometimes I design to express my feelings or moods. For the year and a half that I have been working on these pieces, there is hardly a day that goes by that I am not involved with them in some way."

42. *Untitled No. 2* by Barbara W. Saslow. (left)

43. *Untitled* by Jadine Surette. (top left) "I love antique beads and this needleweaving has been the vehicle for me to integrate the subtleness of silk fibers and the patina of old beads."

44. *Sacred Nymph, After Cranach* by Kathleen Betty Williams. (top right) The Sacred Nymph was designed as a homage to Lucas Cranach the Elder, a 14th-century painter. The low-relief porcelain figure was reproduced and painted by Kathleen. Coupled with a distant landscape and birds the result is an imaginative, almost dreamy piece. Along with needleweaving, the piece also includes knotting and wrapping with embroidery threads.

45. *Sea Fantasy* by Deborah Tweedy. (left) "The integration of beads and fibers satisfies both my passions at once and resolves the frustration created by the limited palette of bead colors. I found this piece to be among the most exciting I have ever created. The colors of 'Sea Fantasy,' are the colors I would like to find under the sea."

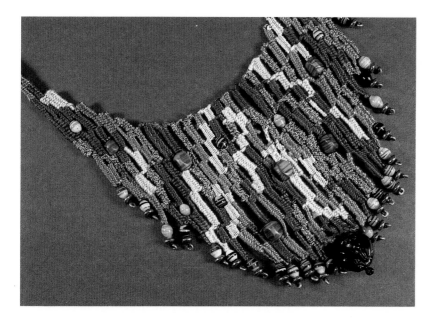

46. *Egyptian Geometry* by Diane Fitzgerald. (top left) "The regularity of Egyptian forms such as the pyramids and their color palette was the starting point for this piece."

47. *Untitled* by Diane Fitzgerald. (top right) "I often wish I had more experience in painting, which I think would make me freer in approaching necklace design. With practice, it's possible to push oneself to new heights."

48. *Monkey Tree* by Diane Fitzgerald. (left) "This piece is all about texture. I tried to create the feeling of tree bark using grays, taupes, beiges and black, and wove the piece at random without a pattern. The large black bead is of a carved monkey."

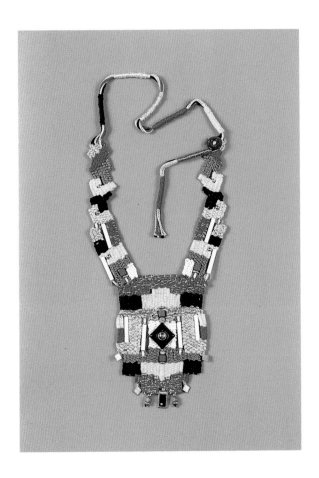

49. *Sun Steps and Shadows* by Daniele S. Dubois. (top left) "This was my third piece, made in Bethesda, Maryland at the end of November 1989. The leaves had fallen, the cold was setting in and the days were shorter. I longed for the wonderful summer I had just spent in the south of France. Gold beads against black onyx...red and gray...the sun of Provence on a scorched land...a stroll in the narrow streets of the old quarter of Nice on a hot Sunday afternoon...sun, steps and shadows."

50. *Africa II* by Carroll Gotte. (top right) "I have always been interested in textiles and more recently have discovered the world of beads. The combining of these interests and study of them in other cultures has been the inspiration for my work. The symbols, materials, designs, colors and use within a culture fascinate me. I find excitement in every phase — learning about the culture, selecting the yarns and beads and in the weaving."

51. *A God's Promise* by Phyllis Magrab. (left)

52. *Pre-Columbian I* **by Carroll Gotte. (top left)**

53. *Bedouin II* **by Carroll Gotte. (top right)**

54. *Pre-Columbian II* **by Carroll Gotte. (left)**

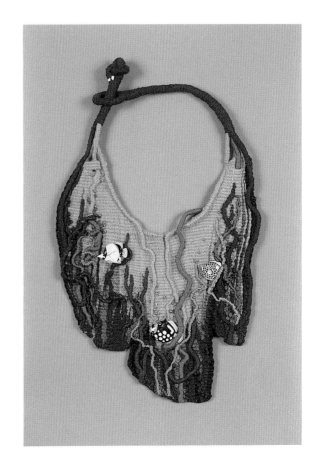

55. *Waterfall* by Sarah Johnson. (top left)

56. *Diver's World* by Sarah Johnson. (top right)

57. *Lepidoptera* by Frances Eyster. (left) "The brass finial is in the shape of a butterfly and its antennae of brass beads lies amidst an ikat-like design also meant to represent the wings of a butterfly."

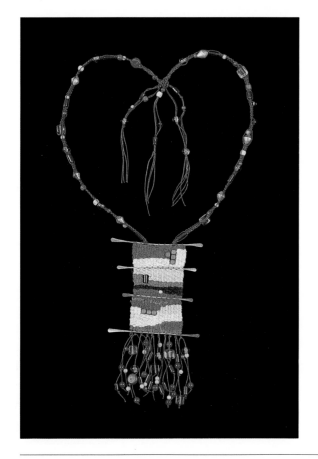

58. *Asian Fantasy* **by Ileen Shefferman. (top left)**

59. *All That Jazz* **by Ileen Shefferman. (top right)**

60. *Ganges* **by Gretchen Prewitt. (left)**

61. *Tapestry Neckpiece with Heart Pendant* by Joan Wack. (top left)

62. *Inca Kilim* by Rebecca Toner. (top right)

63. *Summer's Joy* by Joyce Collin-Bushell. (left) " 'Summer's Joy' began as an exercise while teaching my first workshop in the technique for my guild members. The experience of leading the workshop became very rewarding as I watched the necklaces taking shape. Six of us wore finished necklaces to our annual general meeting in May!"

64. *Untitled No. 1* **by Virginia Hudak. (top left)** "I design my necklaces to provide that unique, dramatic statement for a particular garment or group of separates. The overall design, the color and shape of the beads and ornaments and the color and texture of the threads are all selected quite simply on the basis of how they complement the intended garments.

"The original design usually changes during execution as the beads and threads evolve into an integrated statement. My work reflects my partiality to flowing lines, antique silver and the colors magenta, turquoise and purple."

65. *Untitled No. 3* **by Virginia Hudak. (top right)**

66. *Twenties Angles* **by Eugenia Nowlin. (left)** "Twenties Angles was designed using the Art Nouveau pin in the center as a theme and then working to set it off to best advantage."

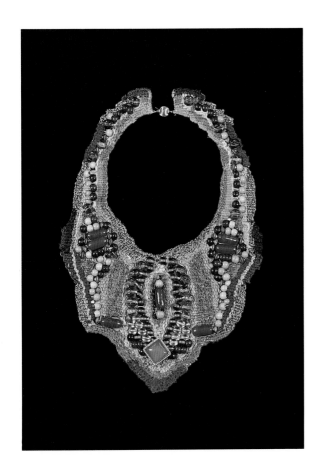

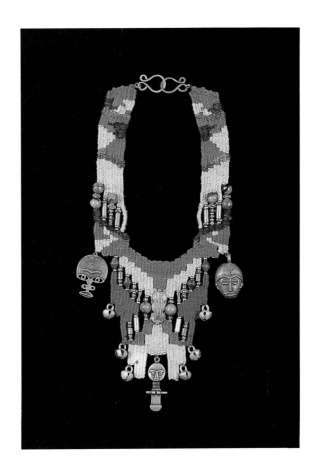

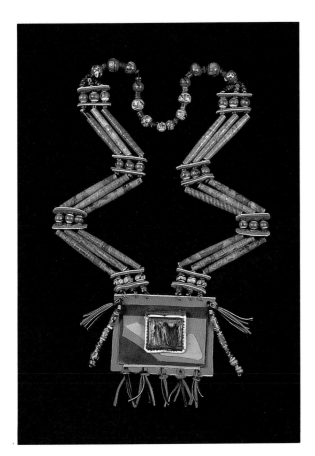

67. *Song of India* by Eugenia Nowlin. (top left)
"The discussion of Indian textiles in Helen's class, and a gift of Indian glass beads from a friend who returned from an inspiring trip through India, resulted in this piece."

68. *Fertility* by Sheila Miller. (top right)

69. *African Adornment* by Eurla Frederick. (left) Note the use of leather and paper beads.

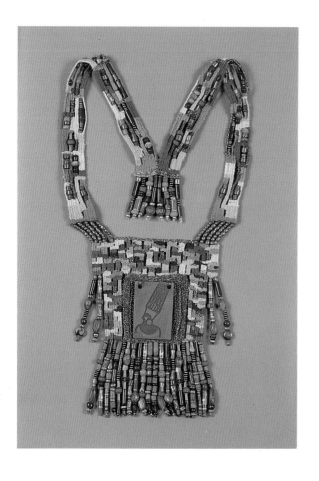

70. *The Egyptian Way* by Eurla Frederick. (top left) The unusual closure adds interest to the back of this piece.

71. *A Puppet Show* by Eurla Frederick. (top right) This pectoral is actually a puppet stage with a metal puppet.

72. *Falling Leaves* by M. A. Klein (left) "My designs for these neckpieces reflect my graphic arts background and training. They also reflect my love of the Southwest and the time I've spent there."

Ms. Klein, whose main interest is fabric collage tapestry, wrote about several experimental pieces she was beginning. These involved unusual warping patterns, such as radial warp, criss-crossed warp, multiple layers of warps and others. Undaunted by the problems of moving into uncharted territory, she tackles them as they confront her and is learning from each as she proceeds.

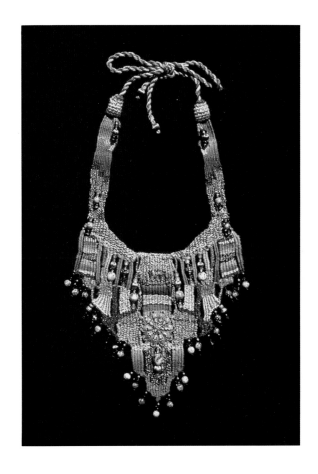

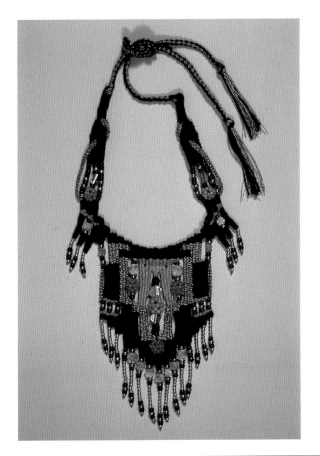

73. *Moonlit Night* **by M. A. Klein. (top left)**

74. *Untitled* **by Rose Madri. (top right)**

75. *Untitled* **by Pat Norman. (left)**

ADVANCED STUDENT WORK

The following photographs typify the range of expression that develops in Helen's specialized or advanced classes. In these classes, Helen explores the textiles and artifacts of a culture with her students and goes deeper into the intricacies of needleweaving. The following necklaces resulted during a special class devoted to Pre-Columbian culture.

76. *Moche, Turquoise and Gold* **by Sheila Miller. (top left) The stepped geometric designs of Peruvian textiles inspired this neckpiece.**

77. *Tumi* **by Sheila Miller. (top right) This piece showcases a replica of an ancient Inca ceremonial knife.**

78. *Untitled* **by Frances Eyster. (left) The Tumi-like elements were forged by Frances who also created the raku beads.**

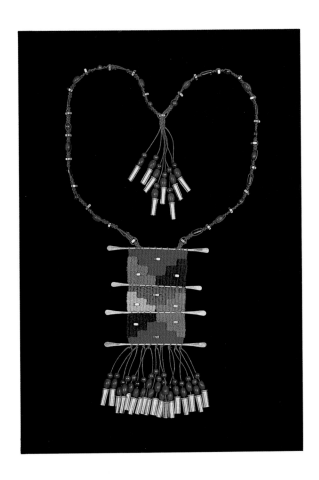

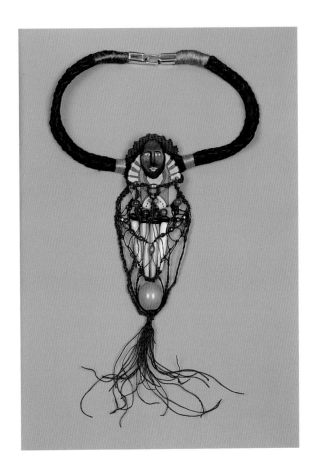

79. *Royal Arsenal* **by Gretchen Prewitt. (top left)**
This piece is based on the geometric weaving
designs of Inca textiles. It also features the brass
shells of a 22-caliber rifle.

80. *Untitled No. 1* **by Jimmylene Wertman. (top**
right) A porcelain fetish and macramé techniques
add to the interest of this piece.

81. *Untitled No. 2* **by Jimmylene Wertman. (left)**
The centerpiece is a museum replica of a gold
bat-man, a Pre-Columbian adornment made by
the lost wax method. Abalone shell elements and
Peruvian beads are also used.

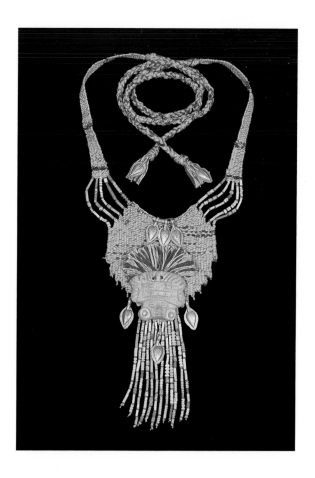

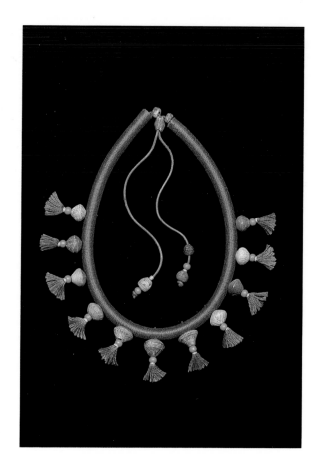

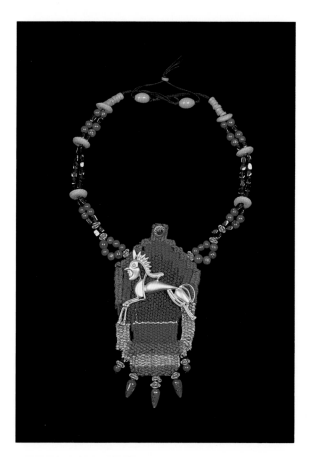

82. *Mayan Mask* by Ileen Shefferman. (top left).

83. *Untitled* by Phyllis Baez. (top right) In their previous incarnation the incised clay whorls on this necklace were used in pre-Columbian civilizations as spindles to spin fiber into thread.

84. *Untitled* by Phyllis Magrab. (left) Golden horse pin on a needlewoven pendant.

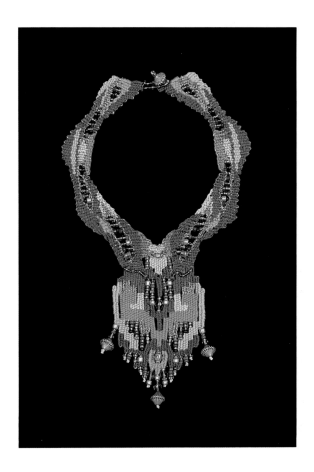

85. *Cam's Frog* by Marion Boyer. (top left) A frog motif was woven within the piece.

86. *Figuratively Feline* by Cookie Labby. (top right) This necklace was warped in two directions. The lower part was warped vertically so that the beads could hang lengthwise. The upper part was warped horizontally so the beads could be arranged horizontally. The colors of beads and threads are typical of Peruvian textiles.

87. *Untitled* by Daniele Dubois. (left) An owl mask with fox ears.

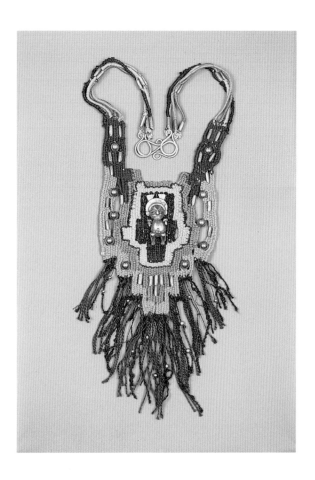

88. *Noble Warrior* by Eugenia Nowlin. (top left) Gold museum replica; multi-strand closure.

89. *Flying Frog* Pectoral by Edward Hyland. (top right) Dangles are of carved stone.

90. *Nazca Huari* Pectoral by Joanne Bast. (left) The design of the interlocking "C's" is derived from the Nazca Huari of the south coast of Peru (ca. 700-1000 AD). This choker style is woven first as a neck band, then the vertical warps are attached to the band to create the pectoral with golden dangles.

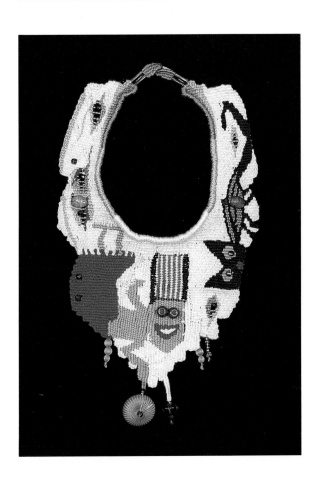

91. *Falling Girl With Cat* by Bonnie Dunn. (left) The falling man motif occurs in pre-Columbian weaving motifs.

92. *Bird Pin* by Maggie Wheeler. (below) "This carving of a bird's head was completed with a needlewoven and beaded body."

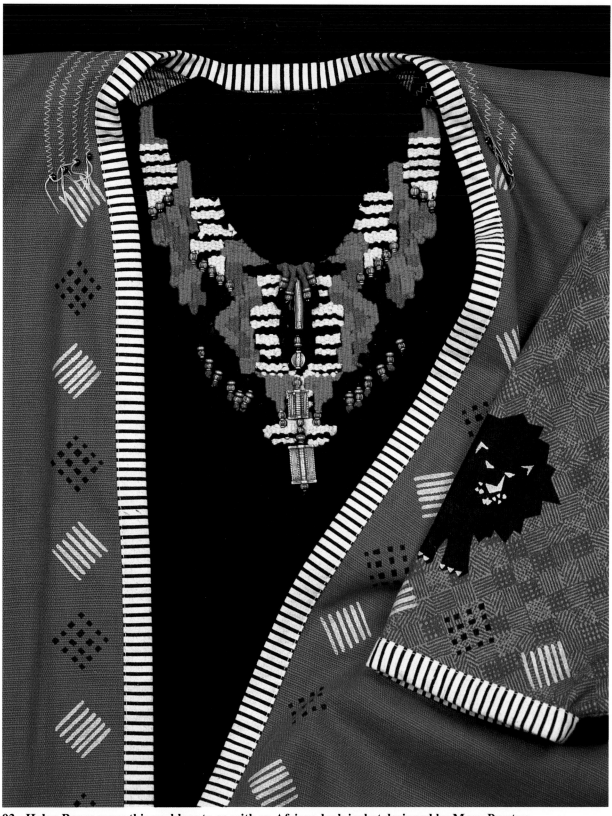

93. Helen Banes wove this necklace to go with an African-look jacket designed by Mary Preston.

Designing Your Own Necklace

Several necklace patterns are included in this book for you to use as they are or for you to modify. Of course, you may want to try designing one of your own. Whatever you decide, this chapter will help you. If you wish to use one of the patterns provided, move right along to Chapter 4: How to Make Your Own Necklace, and come back to this section when you want to make a special necklace with your own design.

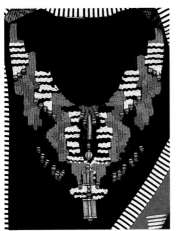

Many people doubt their own creativity. They don't realize that creativity comes a glimpse at a time rather than as a blinding revelation. Each small step we take will eventually bring us to completion of a piece. Often, those people we think are brilliantly creative are building on the work of others. As Thomas Edison said, "Genius is 99% perspiration and 1% inspiration." Look around you for ideas and translate or interpret them into your own designs.

You may wonder how to begin designing a necklace. Like many problems, designing a necklace becomes more manageable when you break it into its component parts. The key elements or building blocks of design with which we will work are color, line, shape, texture and focal point. In working with these elements, it is helpful to have some guidelines for assembling them into a pleasing piece. Three such guidelines are scale, balance and rhythm. These are not meant to be hard and fast rules but rather general ideas to get you started and to help you learn the vocabulary of design. Although not an element of design, we'll also explore symbolism briefly. To begin, let's talk a little about each of these terms and see how they apply to our necklace design.

Just as a child changes as it grows, each piece creates the need for new responses as it evolves. Don't force your original idea during the developing process.

The Building Blocks Of Design: The Elements

Color

Color depends on the composition of the material and how it reflects light. The spectrum of colors we see in a rainbow is merely the beginning of colors available in fibers and beads today. Due to the advances in commercial dyes, fiber artists are fortunate to have a vast assortment of colors readily available. And if commercial colors are not satisfactory, we can create our own by dyeing thread with convenient, color-fast chemical dyes or dyes from natural materials. Beads, too, can have an endless range of color. Beads can be painted or wrapped with thread to achieve an exact color. For more ideas, see Chapter 4: Finding or Making the Perfect Beads for Your Necklace.

Learning to use color seems to come naturally to some people. For others, a more structured approach to understanding color will be easier than trial and error. Many books are available which explain color theory in depth. They describe the color wheel, the composition of colors, the interaction of colors and the meaning of color. We'll give you a brief introduction here.

The Color Wheel

A color wheel represents a method of organizing the colors of the spectrum so that various relationships can be explored. The simplest color wheel shows the primary colors (red, yellow and blue) each spaced at one-third intervals around the wheel. By mixing two of the primaries we get the secondary colors. For example, by mixing red and yellow we get orange, which is placed between red and yellow. Similarly, yellow and blue are mixed to give green, and blue and red are mixed to give purple. Usually a color wheel goes one step further, mixing primary and secondary to achieve tertiary colors. For example, mixing yellow and green gives yellow-green. This gives us a color wheel with twelve colors (see figure 1).

This color wheel is just the beginning of color exploration. There are three aspects to color: the hue or color name; the value, or its lightness or darkness; and the intensity, or how bright or dull it is. Tints of color are made by adding white and shades of color are made by adding black. It is even more exciting to work with colors that are mixtures of many colors. You may wish to try playing with color by mixing colors with inexpensive tempera paints. Start with the basics, black, white, red, yellow and blue.

Color bridges are transitions of color from one value or one hue to another. Light blue to medium blue to dark blue is a transition of

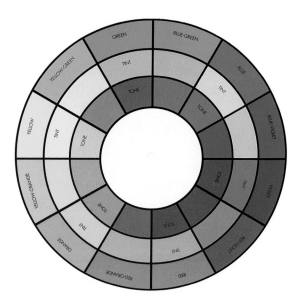

Figure 1. The Color Wheel with Tints and Shades. A color wheel can provide many ideas for color directions. Memorize the sequence of colors and practice recalling their opposites on the wheel (the complementary colors) and their neighbors (the analogous colors). Then think about some neutral colors that could work with your selected color. You'll quickly have several possibilities with which to work. (Courtesy of The Color Wheel, 1337 Donna Beth Ave., West Covina, CA 91791. Manufacturers and distributors of a variety of color wheels.)

value. Such a color scheme would be referred to as "monochromatic." Or, imagine the colors of a glorious sunset, which is a transition of hue. The sky might go from brilliant red-orange to pinks and mauves to the soft gray blue of the evening sky, all with a smooth gradation of colors.

A pleasing color combination can result by selecting colors next to each other on the color wheel, such as blue and green (analogous colors), or by selecting opposite colors, such as orange and blue (complementary colors). More complicated color schemes involve three or more colors such as orange, yellow and blue violet (split complement). Many combinations exist and it's fun to try new colors with which we have not yet worked. When you try using different colors together, note how some colors seem to change in appearance, depending on what other colors are used with them.

Before you start working, ask yourself if you prefer bright, soft, or more neutral colors. Then look at the color wheel. Which color is opposite your selected color on the color wheel? Which color is next to it on either side? Do you have a second or third color choice? Imagine what color might result if you had paint and mixed all these colors together. That color might serve as a bridge between your other colors. By asking yourself questions like these, you can begin to select the colors you would like to work with.

There are many, many color schemes to use. Start with a palette of three or four colors in light, medium and dark values, in monochromatic or contrasting colors. Sometimes adding a touch or highlight of an odd, off-beat color will provide a striking accent to your piece. Restraint is the key here, however.

The best advice I ever heard regarding color was this: Any two colors will work together if you use them with a third color which is a mixture of the two original colors. For example, if you decide to work with yellow and violet, try adding a dull gray-green as your third color. This is the color which would result if you mixed yellow and violet paint. The dull gray-green serves as a transition or bridge between the yellow and violet.

- Diane Fitzgerald

Consider using at least three values — light, medium and dark — so that the necklace can be worn on a variety of background colors. Unlike other art forms which hang on a flat wall or are free standing, wearable art is usually worn against a background which can vary.

- Helen Banes

Often I am inspired to choose a combination of colors for a new piece based on an article of clothing. Since I buy articles for my wardrobe which are made of authentic ethnic textiles or are created by other fiber artists, the necklaces reflect the artistic talent of the original clothing creator. By wearing the necklace with the related clothing, each piece is enhanced. (See Photos 93, (page 32) and 94.)

- Helen Banes

94. This African-inspired necklace was designed by Helen Banes to complement a vest created by Marian Gartler. Marian used a silk african strip weave textile for the vest. The vest is Marian's original "Safe-Keeper" design and features many pockets both inside and out.

Line

A line, my mother told me, is the shortest distance between two points. She remembers this because it was the only question she missed on her high school geometry test. In making necklaces though, we are not concerned about finding the shortest line, but rather the most pleasing line. I like to think of a line as a path which the eye can follow as it moves across your necklace.

A line can be wide or narrow, straight or curved. It can meander or move diagonally. Lines can be solid or a series of dots. In weaving a necklace, a line is created by weaving with thread or by placing a series of beads next to each other. Your eye steps from one bead to another like tiptoeing across stepping stones in a river (figure 2). Lines also serve to define shapes, another element of design.

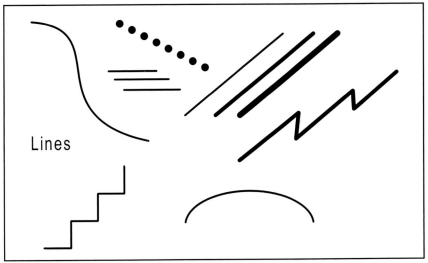

Figure 2. Lines: Lines can provide interesting design possibilities. See the following necklaces for ideas using lines: in photo 39, "Miss Piggy," lines are used to outline shapes. In photo 56, "Diver's World," wavy vertical lines represent undersea vegetation. In photo 71, "Puppet Show," straight lines become stripes.

Try to avoid creating a stripe across the width of the piece, especially a dark or bold stripe which cuts the design in half visually and obstructs the rhythmic movement of the total composition.

- Helen Banes

Although you are using a threaded needle, do not consider the process of needleweaving akin to embroidery or drawing which create a line of color. Needleweaving is more related to the concept of silk screen technique or painting. Consider instead the idea of shapes of color using a combination of beads or a solid area of thread. THINK SHAPES MORE THAN LINES.

- Helen Banes

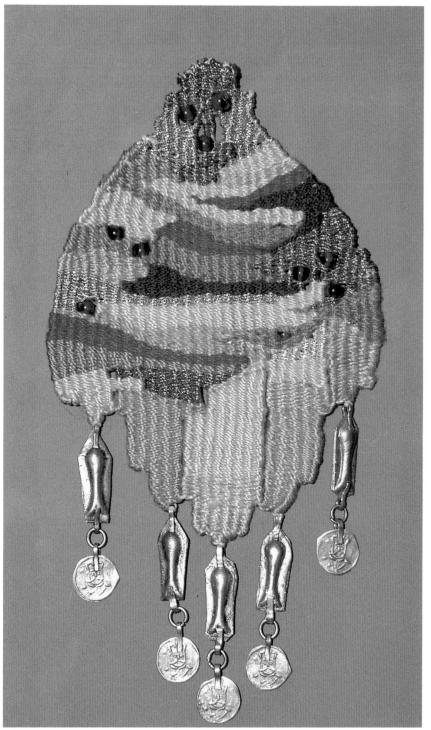

The outline of a hand provides interesting possibilities for designing the outer shape of a necklace. (see photo 95)

- Helen Banes

Another challenge of this design process is the choice between two extremes of composition: one is geometric and balanced design; the other allows shapes of color to flow in an organic way. The symmetrical design is easier and takes a shorter time to complete, whereas an asymmetrical design requires continuous analysis to establish balance and rhythm.

- Helen Banes

95. ***Khamsa #5*** **by Helen Banes is based on a hand shape.**

Shape

Shape is a basic element of design that could also be referred to as form or area. It refers to the two- or three-dimensional aspects of an object and the space it occupies. Shapes may be geometric or free-form. Some familiar geometric shapes are triangles, rectangles, squares, circles, ovals, pentagons, trapezoids and parallelograms. Examples of free-form shapes are amoebae, rocks and the tear drop shape of paisleys. (Figure 3).

Shapes, like color, can convey meaning, arouse emotions and suggest associations to us. Who can think of pyramids without thinking of Egypt? Pentagon has become synonymous with the U.S. Department of Defense because of the five-sided building which this agency occupies in the nation's capitol. Squares suggest rigidity. Rounded forms are soothing. Tall shapes look dignified. Jagged shapes may be exciting. Horizontal shapes are static and restful while diagonal shapes are dynamic and suggest movement. The shapes chosen for weaving a necklace and the beads used will help create the personality of the piece.

Although the overall shape of the necklace is determined by the outline set by the pins and warp, the interior shapes can be modified during the process of weaving. Allowing the design to evolve gives one the pleasure of discovery and is one of the most gratifying joys.

- Helen Banes

Figure 3. Shapes: One way to play with shape to get new ideas is to take a colored picture from a magazine (or simply colored paper) and cut it into various shapes of different sizes. Practice arranging these in new ways on a contrasting or similar background. When you find a particularly pleasing arrangement, try using it in a necklace.

Texture

Texture refers to the surface appearance of the necklace, including the beads and threads. It can be both seen and felt and contributes to the overall look and feel of the piece. One of the delights of needle-woven jewelry is the contrast between soft, flexible threads and shiny glass or metal beads. In general, smooth textures are more formal and rougher textures more informal. The type of weaving used in needle-woven jewelry results in a texture even when using the smoothest threads. Fortunately, we have a wide range of thread available to us with almost any texture we might imagine. The fine metallic threads and even ordinary sewing thread can be woven along with a rougher thread to change the texture and color. Be careful of very nubby threads, though. They are difficult to weave because they do not slide easily across the warp threads.

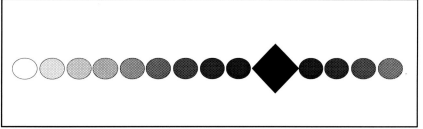

Figure 4. Focal Point: This is the most important feature of your necklace. It is where the eye comes to rest in viewing the piece.

Focal Point

The focal point is the most important part of your necklace. It creates emphasis in a certain area to attract the eye and accent your piece. A focal point can be created with a special bead, a group of beads, a button, a buckle, an unusual object or an area of weaving which will be the dominant part of the necklace. Of course, for one part to be dominant, other parts should be subordinate and assume less prominence. Your focal point can be given more attention by accenting it with a small amount of a contrasting color, by creating lines which draw the eye toward it, or by surrounding it with a shape which contrasts or complements the shape of the focal point. I like to think of the focal point as the "home plate." When your eye sweeps across your piece, it pauses and rests at the focal point (see figure 4). The focal point is critical in defining the overall personality of your piece. For example, if you have an elaborate glass or metal bead, it could be the starting point for designing a necklace with related beads and threads that enhance it.

By employing metallic threads in needle-weaving you can enhance the jewel-like quality of your designs.

- Helen Banes

The contrast between the soft, flexible textural quality of the threads and the hard, shiny, transparent quality of the beads provides the most stimulating challenge in creating a design.

- Helen Banes

A jewelry effect is immediately achieved when a brooch or a combination of beads are used as a focal point.

- Helen Banes

How To Design Using The Elements

Now let's see how we can design a necklace by organizing the elements of color, line, shape, texture and focal point using scale, balance and rhythm.

Scale

Scale, or proportion, refers to the way a part or parts relate to the whole. In making a necklace there are two aspects of scale we should consider. The first is the proportion of the design elements (shapes) which combine to make up the necklace. If your shapes and beads are small, they will be lost when viewed at a distance and will appear simply as texture. If they are large, you will have a bold design. For your first necklace, vary the sizes of your shapes from small to large. The second aspect is the proportion of the necklace to the size and shape of the wearer, particularly the wearer's face. For a person with a large frame, the necklace should be proportionately larger, while a smaller necklace would be appropriate for a smaller person. Since the necklace is worn close to the face, use a shape that is flattering to the face. Remember also that a new shape will be created if your necklace is worn quite low below the collar bone. The supports for the weaving (the part that goes around the neck) can outline a new shape.

A good way to preview the shape and scale of a design is to cut a paper pattern and hold it up to yourself in the mirror. To make a symmetrical necklace, fold the paper in half and cut both sides at the same time.

Balance

When we think about balance, the familiar balance scale comes to mind. Balance for a necklace refers to the visual weight of one side compared to the other side. One way to achieve balance is to make both sides exactly the same—one side is the mirror image of the other. This is referred to as symmetry or formal balance. Since both sides are exactly equal, everything is in balance, so to speak.

Another kind of balance is informal balance or asymmetry. In this case, both sides appear to have the same visual weight, even though the two sides are not mirror images of each other. Your focal point may be placed in the center, and subordinate parts may or may not be the same on both sides. However, their visual weight should be about equal so that it doesn't appear that the necklace is heavier on one side than the other. If you place your focal point off center, you may want a point of interest on the opposite side, either smaller beads or woven shapes, to balance the piece.

Horizontal lines are static, whereas diagonal lines create dynamic movement. Hans Hoffman, the painter of brilliant color abstractions, emphasized the need for a 'push/pull' effect in his art. Keep this in mind to avoid a design that is unexciting. My first painting teacher advised, 'Don't go for the expected, safe solution, choose the most challenging one.'

- Helen Banes

Rhythm

We recognize the concept of rhythm from music and dance. Rhythm is created by the interaction of all the elements. Like rhythm in music, rhythm is used to create a regular harmonious pattern or motion within the piece. Rhythm can be achieved in several ways. One way is to repeat elements such as lines or shapes. Another way is to graduate colors, going from light to dark, or graduate shapes, going from large to small (figure 5).

Still another way to achieve rhythm is to group beads together to create a new shape. Grouping beads is one of the most important ways of creating rhythm in a necklace. When beads are placed close together in a group, they take on added importance. From a distance, a group of beads appears as a unit with a new shape. On closer inspection, each bead is distinct. This adds to the enjoyment of the necklace (figure 6).

Figure 5. Rhythm: Just like the beat of a marching band, repeating patterns can impart rhythm to a necklace.

Using beads of similar shapes and color can become monotonous, like a Johnny-One-Note song compared to a sonata or symphony. Consider beads of a variety of shapes so that the long, narrow beads, or a line of small beads, can balance on either side of a large round bead.

- Helen Banes

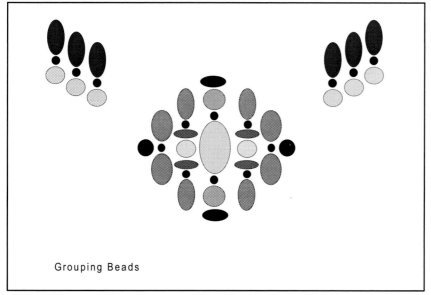

Grouping Beads

Figure 6. Grouping Beads to Create New Shapes: Take the time to explore and enjoy this fascinating aspect of necklace design. Have a variety of beads in different shapes and colors on hand when you begin. Try laying the beads on a cloth to keep them from rolling, or temporarily string them on a wire to hold them in place, while you consider the merits of your arrangement and try other related arrangements. The beads should fit together so they don't crowd each other and distort the design.

Symbolism

Although symbolism is not an element of design, some people enjoy incorporating symbols into the objects they create. A short discussion of symbolism may inspire you to explore this rich area for ideas for creating a necklace or other needlewoven accessories.

When we talk about symbolism, we are referring to the meaning of an object beyond what is immediately obvious to the viewer. Symbolism requires an interpretation by the viewer. In other words, the viewer's understanding or experience affects her appreciation of the object. For example, flags are symbols which convey meaning. Groups of people create a flag to symbolize their group or nation. In many cultures, beads serve as symbols in a similar way. In the United States, Camp Fire Girls earn beads for various accomplishments. Wearing a particular bead conveys to all other Camp Fire Girls that the individual has performed a particular task. Among a southern African tribe, the Ndebele, a ritual of bead adornment marks each phase of life from birth to death. Other objects and shapes can also convey meaning.

Every object reflects the values, views and traditions of the person or people who produced it. To interpret a culture we must try to understand the philosophy of the people or the period. How do they place themselves in relation to the rest of the world? What are their beliefs, customs and rituals, and how are these portrayed in their work? Do they value handwork? In some cultures, symbolic items are used only during feasts, ceremonies or occasions, while in other cultures, they are used as everyday items as reminders of something important.

If we wish to, we can create symbolism in a necklace by using commonly understood symbols. If we make a red, white and blue necklace, it is likely to symbolize patriotism in this country. If we use a heart shape, it will symbolize love. Some examples of symbolic shapes from other cultures or periods are shown in this section.

By working on a series of pieces based on a specific culture, I find that each piece becomes stronger as it builds on the previous experience. After steeping myself in references and examples of the artifacts, I need more than one example to express my response to the inspiration.

- Helen Banes

Ancient Egyptian Motifs, Materials and Colors

Motifs: Eye of Horus, scarab, ankh, winged falcon, lotus and papyrus, sun disk and crescent moon, Djed pillar, vulture's head, cobra (upright).

Materials: Gold, copper, lapis lazuli, obsidian, glass (colored and opaque) faience*, carnelian, turquoise, quartz, chalcedony.

Colors: Moss green, black, cream, dull orangey red, turquoise blue, yellow ochre.

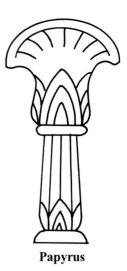

Papyrus

Winged Falcon

Lotus Blossom

Eye of Horus

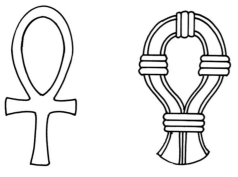

Two Types of Ankh Symbols

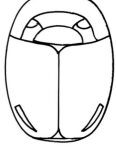

Scarab

Figure 7. _____

*Powdered quartz heated until fused, coated with blue, green, yellow or white glaze.

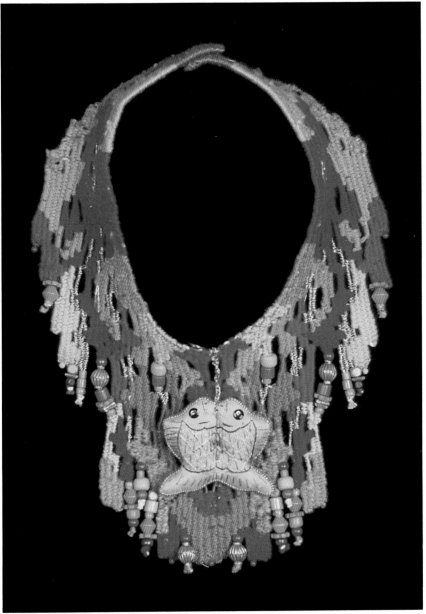

Jade, the mineral nephrite, had a special significance in ancient China. It was not only valued as a precious and beautiful stone but was believed to have spiritual and even magical qualities. Many Chinese carvings are in the shapes of animals and were pierced so that they might be attached to clothing or worn as pendants.

This necklace incorporates the ancient Chinese symbol of double fish as the focal point of the piece .

96. *Peking Opera.* **Necklace with a Chinese double fish-pendant as the focal point. Necklace by Helen Banes.**

Ancient Chinese Motifs, Materials and Colors

Motifs in Design: Yin and Yang, floral imagery, bats and butterflies, calligraphic designs and animals of the Zodiac.

The Eight Buddhist Symbols of Happy Augury

Double Fish — abundance and marital fidelity

Endless Knot — eternity and the everlasting love of Buddha

Lotus — purity; the flower rises from turbid water untarnished

Sacred Vase — peace and the water of life

Canopy — shelter for all living things

Conch Shell — signal to worship

State Umbrella — symbolizes an incorruptible official

Wheel of Law — the ever-turning cycle of life

Canopy

Materials: jade, ivory, lacquer, cloisonné, carved wood, glass, turquoise, coral, carved seeds and pits, painted porcelain and cinnabar.

Colors:

Yellow, which was worn only by royalty, symbolizes the earth.

Red, represents the element fire and is used at weddings and births.

Black, associated with winter and the elderly, is symbolized by a tortoise.

White, a color traditionally worn for funerals and mourning, signifies the tiger.

Blue, the symbol of the dragon, is related to spring.

Butterfly

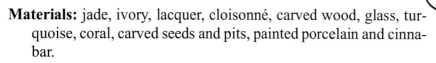

Lotus

Double Fish

Figure 8.

Umbrella

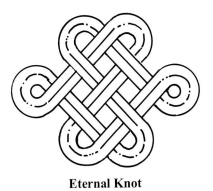

Eternal Knot

Wheel

Dragon

Conch Shell

Vase

Figure 9.

Native American Motifs, Materials and Colors

Motifs: sun, thunderbird, birds, flowers, geometric shapes, stars, snakes, animals.

Materials: leather, feathers, wool, reed and grasses, fur, wood, glass and clay beads, turquoise, pottery, horn, dew claws, quills, silver, copper.

Colors: black, white, red, yellow, blue, turquoise, silver.

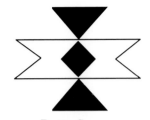

Butterfly: Everlasting Life

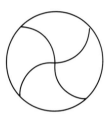

Four Ages: Baby, Youth, Adult and Elder

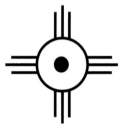

Sun: Happiness

Morning Stars: Guidance

Medicine Man's Eye: Watchful and Wise

Mountains: Abundance

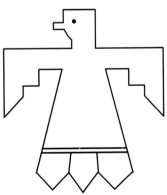

Thunderbird: Happiness

Time: Days and Nights

Figure 10.

Pre-Columbian Motifs, Materials and Colors

Motifs: human figures with hands raised, monkey-like creatures, fish, toads and tadpoles representing water, plumed serpents, pumas, alligators, two-headed felines, stylized birds, and llamas.

Materials: gold, associated with the sun; silver, associated with the moon; tumbaga, an alloy of gold and copper; copper, pottery (in the form of spindle whorls), feathers, Spondylus shell, from the spiny oyster, jade, obsidian, turquoise, chrysacolla (similar to turquoise), amethyst and emeralds.

Colors: blue from indigo, rich carmine from cochineal insects, black, white, jade green, terra-cotta, and mustard gold.

Gold was lavishly used in Inca society for jewelry of all types, including pectorals, rings, armbands and headdresses. It also adorned thrones and walls. King Atahualpa, an Incan leader who, in full regalia of gold ornaments and brightly colored feathers, met the Spanish explorer Francisco Pizarro when he landed in 1532, was amazed that these adventurers would seek gold when they already had beads made of glass.

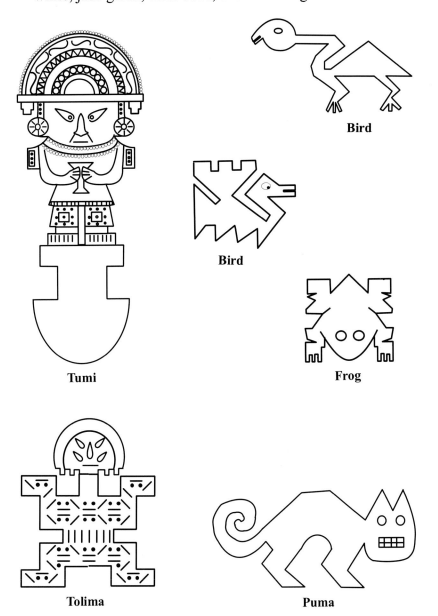

Tumi

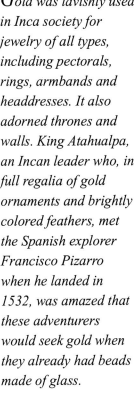

Bird

Bird

Frog

Tolima

Puma

Stylized Human Figure

Figure 11.

Art Deco Motifs, Materials and Colors

Motifs: rising sun, radiating and telescoping lines; flight and winged creatures; deer; stylized flowers; bold geometric, mechanized, streamlined or cubist shapes; horizontal bars; bubbles. These motifs, in turn, were influenced by Native American, Egyptian, Aztec and African designs.

Materials: chrome, off-white and black lacquer, glass, silver, cloisonné, jade, pearl, coral, plastic, ivory, ebony, rhinestones and other semi-precious faceted colored stones, crystal.

Colors: cream, soft coral red, jade green, silver, black lacquer.

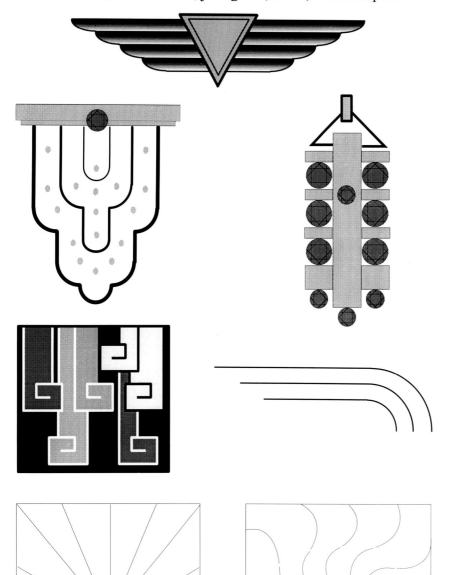

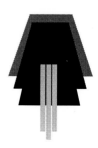

Figure 12.

Style: Bringing It All Together!

The way the elements of design are combined creates what we call "style." How do we describe style? We do so by considering all the design elements just discussed. The Art Deco style, for example, is noted for its strong geometric shapes; its colors, such as cream, coral, jade green, silver, black lacquer; and its textures which are smooth and shiny. Your piece will reflect your own personal style as well.

For some people, it helps if they name their piece before they start. This gives them a goal or focus for their work. One student named her piece "New York, New York," and used black, red, white and crystal beads and black, red and silver thread. She said that whenever she was tempted to add another color, she knew it would only detract from the look she was after. By maintaining her focus she created a striking piece.

Once you understand the basic principles of design, you might want to look at the work of artists, nature or cultures other than your own for ideas and inspiration. A good way to begin is to become aware of characteristic colors, materials, shapes and symbols in the artifacts of a particular culture or artistic period. Borrow books from your library and page through them. You might begin to recognize stylized birds or flowers, symbolic representations of religious icons, abstract shapes such as circles or triangles, certain curves or lines. When you have found a style that appeals to you, define it according to the elements we have described and then use those descriptions to begin your necklace design.

To design a pleasing, well integrated necklace, all the elements of design—the colors, beads, shapes and texture—must be unified and harmonious.

- Diane Fitzgerald

Drawing Your Own Pattern

You can begin your own pattern by drawing the outer shape first (see figure 14), and then filling in with smaller shapes or by drawing smaller shapes, and filling in the background or overall outline last. When you have your pattern worked out, transfer it to graph paper, (one-quarter inch graph paper works the best), centering the pattern on the center line of your sheet.

To help you keep track of which pair of warp threads you are working with later, it is advisable to number the location of each pin. When you have the pattern transferred, mark the placement of pins as follows: Across the **top** of the pattern, place a pin marker **midway between** the vertical graph lines wherever your pattern outline crosses a column of squares. On the **bottom** of the pattern, place a pin marker **on the graph line** wherever the pattern outline crosses graph lines (see figure 13).

Number the pins as follows: Across the top, begin at the center of your graph paper and number the pin markers outward in both directions, e.g.,

9 8 7 6 5 4 3 2 1 1 2 3 4 5 6 7 8 9

Across the bottom, again number the pin markers outward in both directions. Note, however, that you will now have a "0" at the center line for the center pin:

9 8 7 6 5 4 3 2 1 0 1 2 3 4 5 6 7 8 9

Check to be certain that there is only one pin marker in each space between graph lines and only one pin marker on each graph line.

You may color your pattern or merely indicate which colors you will use in each space. (see figure 16)

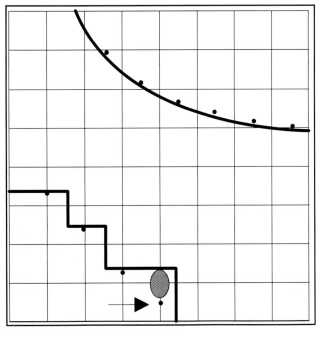

Figure 13. Pin Placement. After drawing your pattern, mark the edges where the pins will be placed as follows: On the top edge of the pattern, place the marks halfway between the vertical lines wherever your pattern line crosses a column of squares. On the bottom of your pattern, place the marks on the vertical lines.

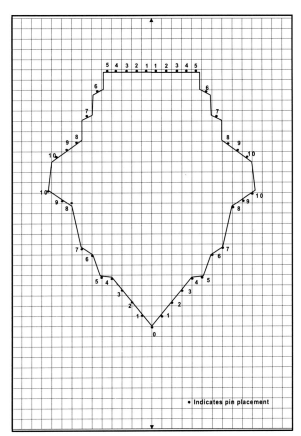

Figure 14. Necklace outline transferred to graph paper with dots indicating pin placement and pin numbers.

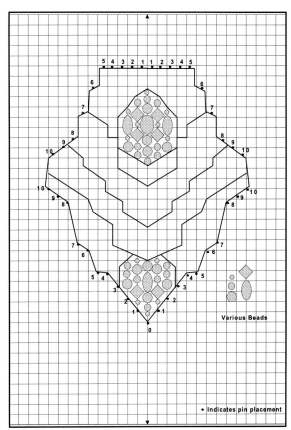

Figure 15. Necklace pattern with beads and areas of weaving drawn in.

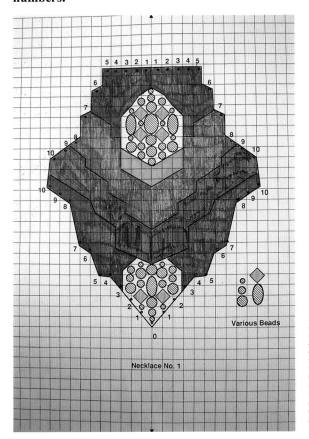

Figure 16. A fully colored pattern helps you see how your colors will work together and whether there is appropriate balance and proportion. Place tracing paper over a colored pattern if you use it on the weaving board to keep it from smudging onto your yarns or copy your pattern without color and use a color key to indicate areas of color.

97. *Song of India* No. 2 by Helen Banes.

Weaving Your Necklace

In this chapter we'll discuss the tools and supplies needed, how to string the warp on a working board, adding beads, weaving with a needle and finishing techniques.

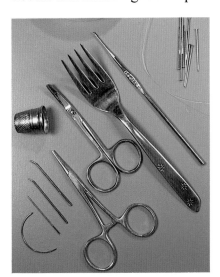

Tools And Supplies

In anticipation of starting your necklace, gather together the following items:

Graph Paper: a quarter-inch grid.

Tracing Paper

Board: A 9" x 12" board or one large enough to extend at least one inch beyond all sides of the piece. Homosote board available at lumber yards, sometimes called bulletin board, insulation board or ceiling tile, is a good choice and it can be used several times. Foam core, available at art supply stores, should be used in two layers. It is not as strong as homosote board and it does not hold the pins as firmly. Wood is too dense to insert pins into easily.

Tape: If you use homosote board, cover the back and sides of it with two-inch masking tape or duct tape to prevent it from flaking. Also use masking tape to hold the pattern in place.

Straight Pins: Although regular pins will hold, they tend to bend easily. Super-plated, #17 or #20 gauge, 1-1/2" steel pins are recommended. They are available at office supply stores as bank pins. T-pins and push pins catch the thread when weaving and can be frustrating to work with.

Headpins: Headpins are short wires on which beads are strung. They look like blunt pins and can be bought wherever jewelry parts are sold.

Warp Thread: Warp threads form the structure of the piece and carry the beads which are strung onto them. I usually use an 18-gauge, three-ply, waxed linen carpet thread as my warp. I prefer it because it is heavy enough to support the beads, it gives structure to your piece and it is less likely to be split by the needle when you weave. (See Supplies section for sources.) Any color warp may be used because it is almost completely covered in the weaving process. For lighter pieces, however, it is desirable to use a light-color warp and for darker pieces a black or brown warp. If your beads have small holes try using a lighter weight thread. Do not use monofilament line for the warp thread because it results in a very stiff piece that will not drape to fit the contour of the body.

Weft or Weaving Thread: No. 3 Perle Cotton is an ideal yarn to weave with. Other cotton threads designed for knitting will also work, as will pearl rayon, silk or synthetic thread of similar weight. Metallic threads of varying weights add sparkle and may be used alone or with other thread. (Photo 98.)

Scissors: A small needlework scissors

Needles: Use #18, #20 or #22 tapestry needles for weaving. These work best because their points are somewhat rounded and they are less likely to split the warp thread. Some people like to bend the tip of their needle slightly to make the weaving process easier. Many #20 needles can be bent without heating. If you wish to do this, wear safety glasses or hold the pliers and your needle under a table when bending it, just in case the needle breaks. Hold the needle in your hand. Use your pliers to bend the tip of the needle about 1/4 inch from the end at an angle of about 30. Some needles need to have their temper removed in order to make them less brittle. To do this, hold the needle with your pliers and heat the needle until it is red hot. Plunge the red-hot needle into cold water to cool. Bend as described.

There may be tight places where it will be difficult to weave. A curved needle, about 1.5" from tip to tip, works well here. Curved needles with a tapestry point are rather difficult to find. However, curved upholstery needles are readily available. You may also be able to obtain surgical needles, which come in a variety of sizes. Dull the sharp points with a file or sand paper.

Needle-nosed pliers or a hemostat: (Optional) Needle-nosed pliers can be used to grab the needle in tight places and do what big fingers sometimes cannot. An alternative to the pliers is a hemostat, a medical tool similar to a small forceps with fine-pointed ends and handles that lock into place. You may find them at drugstores, hospital supply outlets or flea markets. Eyebrow tweezers, available at cosmetic counters, are another alternative.

A student inquired, "What is the meaning of the word, 'warp?'" I discovered the original meaning from Old English is "to throw or cast." What I originally considered a foolish question gave me a better understanding of the term.

- Helen Banes

98. No. 3 Perle Cotton is the ideal weight for weaving. Other rayon, linen, silk, synthetic and metallic threads of similar weight may also be used.

Beater (Table Fork): To beat the weft threads (pack them tightly together), use a small, pronged device such as a table fork or a comb with teeth 1/4" apart. To begin with, any table fork will do. Later you may want to substitute a fancier fork or other implement. It will make weaving just that much more fun!

Beads: Beads of any material may be used, including glass, plastic, metal, bone, polymer clay, ceramic or shell. They must have a hole large enough to slide onto the warp thread and typically should be less than 1/2" diameter in order to fit between the warp threads within the weaving. Somewhat larger beads can be used at the ends of warp threads, but plan to leave space around them so that they hang freely. You may also use buttons, bells, buckles, netsuke or ojime (antique carved Japanese miniature figures with holes), medallions, or any other perforated item.

Warp Endings: Warp threads which have beads at their very ends require some means of preventing the beads from coming off. Crimps (small circles of soft metal), heishi (tiny rings of metal or shell), shank buttons, charms, links from a chain, rings and many other items can be attached to the end of a warp.

Bead Threader: A six-inch piece of monofilament fishing line is convenient for stringing beads on the warp threads. A crochet hook (size 12 or 13) will also work if the bead holes are large enough.

Fray Prevention: For metallic threads that tend to fray, a light application of clear fingernail polish can be used to glue fibers together and prevent their fraying. Alternatively, there are commercial sewing aids such as "Fray Check" which also serve this purpose.

Stringing Your Warp Onto The Working Board

You've already chosen a pattern from the previous chapter or have drawn one yourself. Now it's time to get started. Take one step at a time and you'll soon be weaving. Tape your graph paper pattern to the board. Each column of squares on the graph paper will indicate where a pair of warp threads will be placed. If you have colored your pattern, you may wish to place a piece of tracing paper over it to protect your thread from color on the pattern paper rubbing off. (Photo 99)

Insert pins at the points marked earlier on your drawing. Pins should be placed at an oblique angle, about 30-45°, slanting them toward the top at the top of the piece and toward the bottom at the bottom of the piece (in other words, away from the design). (See figure 17.) Note that you'll have an uneven number of pins across the bottom and an even number of pins across the top. Check to be sure that the pins are placed correctly. Remember that pins across the top go between the graph paper lines and across the bottom, go on the lines.

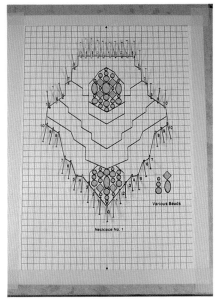

99. Tape your pattern to the working board. If your board has a tendency to flake, then tape the edges and back of your working board, too.

Figure 17. Angle of pin placement

With the warp still on the spool, make a slip knot with a 1/4" loop in the end of the thread. It is important to leave this loop because you will weave into the loop later to secure the end of the warp. Leave a 3-4" tail. (See figure 18.)

Slip this loop onto the outermost pin on the left. Wrap back and forth around the pins going from top to bottom. The warp should be fairly tight so that there is a little tension on the thread, but still have some flexibility. (See figure 20.)

When you have strung the warp around all the pins, make another slip knot and attach it to the last pin on the right side, again leaving a 1/4" loop and 3-4" tail and pull the thread taut. Clip the thread from the spool. (Photo 100.)

Neckedge: On necklaces with curved necklines, you may wish to make a smoother edge than the stair-stepped edge that will result from your normal weaving. To make this smooth edge, attach an extra thread to the innermost top pin with a slip knot, then string it through the tops of the warp pairs and attach it to the opposite top pin with a slip knot. Be sure to weave through these knots to secure them. (See Figure 19.)

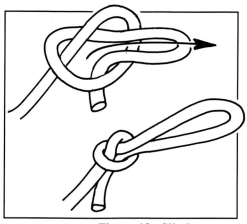

Figure 18. Slip knot

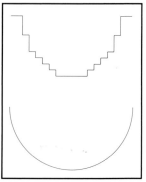

Figure 19. Neckline Edge Options. Above: Stair neck edge. Below: Smooth neck edge.

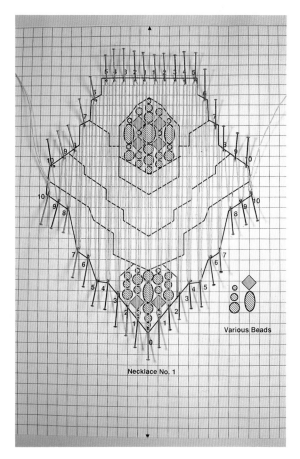

Necklace No. 1

Various Beads

100. Place a pin at each pin marker. Pins across the top should be slanted toward the top of the working board; pins across the bottom, should slant toward the bottom. Tie a slip knot at the end of the warp thread while it is still on the spool. Tie your warp to the outer most pin on the left with a slip knot, wrap the warp back and forth around the pins, going from top to bottom. When you reach the farthest pin on the right, tie your warp to it. You may have to move that last pin slightly to maintain the proper tension after you have tied your warp to it.

Warp and Weft: The warp threads are strung onto the loom first, either horizontally or vertically. They form the skeleton or structure of your piece. The weft threads are woven over and under the warp, usually perpendicular to the warp. All of the warp will be covered with the weft threads.

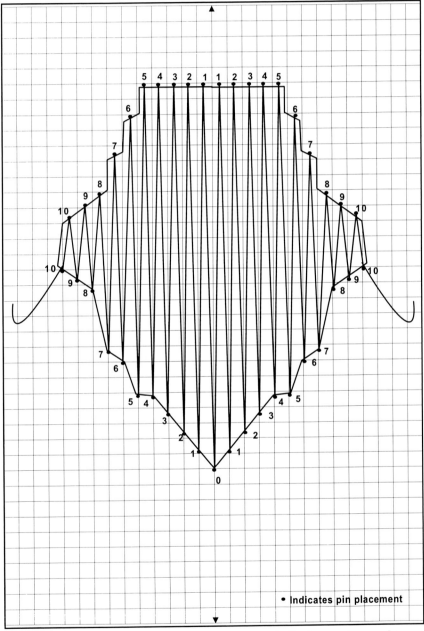

Figure 20. Diagram showing the warp strung onto the loom with marks and numbers for pin placement.

Usually I work on several pieces at a time, alternating between a piece I have on my workboard and arranging beads for a possible necklace or bracelet. Being playful with loose beads relaxes my fingers and restores my ability to concentrate so that I can return to the fiber design with a fresh approach.

- Helen Banes

Adding Beads

The beads you use and how you arrange them can turn an ordinary necklace into a magnificent one. It's worth trying different arrangements before you settle on the one you know will be best for the necklace. It's easy to try different arrangements by holding your beads in place on headpins. (Photo 101.)

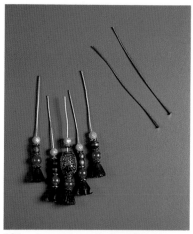

101. Arrange your beads on a wire or headpin to see how the various combinations will look. Take time to try many different arrangements to find the one most pleasing to you.

All beads are strung onto the warp threads before weaving; they are not sewn on later. Usually beads are strung on from the bottom, although you may string them on from the top also. To string the beads onto the warp, use either the monofilament line or a crochet hook as follows:

1. Use the monofilament line if a crochet hook will not go through the hole in your beads. First remove the pin from the bottom of the pair of warp threads on which you intend to string the beads. (The bead closest to the top of the necklace goes on first.) Put the piece of monofilament line between the warp threads, then bring the two ends of the monofilament line together. Now pass both ends of the monofilament through the bead. Slide the bead from the monofilament line onto the warp threads. Add one bead at a time. (Photo 102.) When all the beads are on, remove the monofilament.

2. A second way to string the beads onto the warp is by using a crochet hook. After removing the pin from a pair of warp threads, slip the hook through the bead, hook the crochet hook onto the pair of warp threads and slip the bead from the hook onto the warp. (Photo 103.)

Replace the pin after all the beads are strung on that pair of warp threads. (Photo 104.)

If you have an unusual piece such as a buckle or a button, slide it onto the warp face down and keep the warp threads on top of it. You will be working on the back of your necklace. Weave completely across the back, covering the item with weaving so that it will stay in place. If the item is very thick you may want to carve a depression in your board where the piece will be located so that the weaving will lie flat.

If you have not previously indicated bead placement on your pattern, now put a pencil mark on the pattern at the top and bottom of each column of beads so that you can move the beads out of the way when weaving. Reposition your beads as you are ready to weave them in.

I usually start weaving at the top of the piece so that I can add additional elements from the lower end. I simply remove the pin and slide the beads on or off the unwoven end of the warp.

Allow yourself the pleasure of being playful with assembling the beads on the warp. Moving and rearranging the beads to create interesting patterns is fun and can change the original plan. This can even be done as the weaving progresses.

- Helen Banes

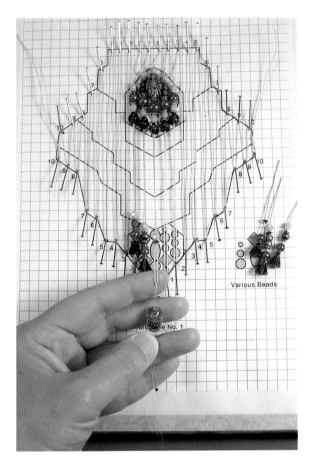

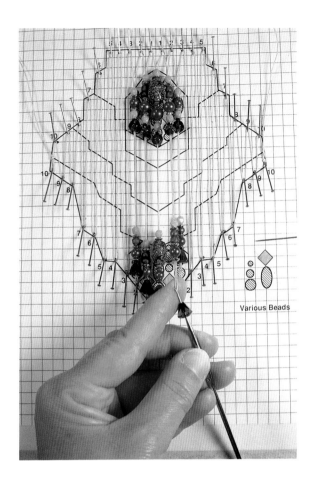

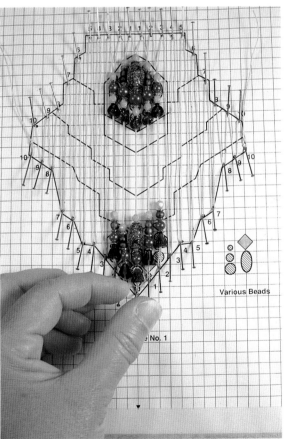

102. (top left) Stringing beads onto the warp using monofilament line: Remove the pin at the bottom of the pair of warp threads on which you plan to string your beads. Pass one end of a short piece of monofilament line between the pair of warp threads and bring the two ends of the line together. Pass these two ends of line through the bead and slip the bead from the line to the warp.

103. (top right) Stringing beads onto the warp using a crochet hook: Remove the pin at the bottom of the pair of warp threads on which you plan to string your beads. Slip the bead onto a crochet hook, then catch the warp pair with the crochet hook and slip the bead from the hook to the warp.

104. Replace the pin after you have strung all the beads on that pair of warp threads.

Finishing The Ends Of The Warp Threads

Only warp pairs with beads on the ends require finishing; other warp pairs can simply be woven together. If you have beads at the end of your warp, you must leave sufficient warp for this finishing.

The ends of the warp thread pairs may simply be woven together without embellishment or you may add beads to resemble a fringe. Beads at the ends of warp threads can add movement to the necklace so consider this in your design. You need not finish the ends before you start weaving. You might want to change your bead arrangement later while you're weaving. Once you're sure of your bead placement, go ahead and finish the ends.

Here are some ways to keep beads from coming off the ends. You may think of others.

1. Perforated ornaments: Small flat beads such as African heishi beads (about 1/16" in diameter), shank buttons, washers, open coins or other flat pieces with holes in them can be attached to the bottom of warp threads to keep end beads from sliding off. When stringing the warp, you will need to allow extra length for the warp thread in order to attach the object. Usually this is a little more than double the length from the top of the object to its hole. (Figure 21.)

To attach these perforated ornaments, remove the pin at the bottom of a warp pair and slip the object onto the warp threads. Open the loop at the bottom, then slip the loop back over the object. (Some people refer to this as a "sales tag" knot, while weavers call it a "lark's head" knot.) Replace the pin.

2. Crimps: Crimps are tiny circles of soft gold or silver metal which can be flattened with a pliers. They are usually used when securing a clasp to a necklace. Slip one onto the end of a pair of warp threads, then carefully squeeze it with a pliers to flatten. This finish is suggested for more formal pieces and gives a little sparkle to the ends. (Photo 105.)

3. Knots of thread: Take a small piece of thread in a color that will work with the design, fold it in half, slip the folded end through the end of a warp pair and pass the ends of the thread through the loop to form a sales tag knot. Add a drop of white glue to the knot. When dry, clip off the ends. It will be secure. This method is suggested for more casual or folk-inspired pieces. If you are using a bead just above these knots, choose a bead with a small hole so that it will not slip off the finishing knot.

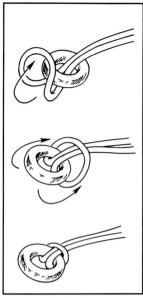

Figure 21. Sales tag or lark's head knot

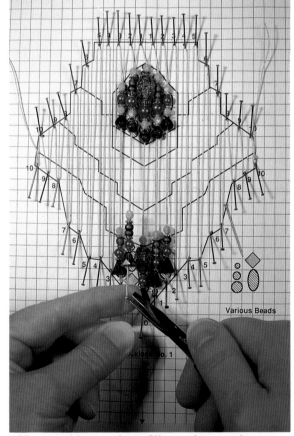

Various Beads

105. Attaching a crimp: Slip a crimp on the warp pair with monofilament line, as if it were a bead. Before removing the line, flatten the crimp around the warp by squeezing it with pliers. Note: Once a crimp has been flattened against the warp, it is very difficult to remove, so be sure of your bead placement before fastening the crimp.

Weaving With A Needle

Now we're ready to begin weaving. This type of weaving is referred to as "weft-faced" weaving, meaning that the weaving or weft thread completely covers the warp.

Begin weaving at the uppermost part of your necklace so that beads can still be added at the lower edge or changed later, if necessary.

Thread your needle with about 24" of the weft or weaving thread you wish to use for that area. Lay the tail of your thread along the edge warp thread and weave around it as though it were part of the first warp thread. It is not necessary to make a knot. (Photo 106.)

When weaving, each warp thread is treated individually. Go under the first warp thread and over the second one of each pair and so on across the area to be filled. Now in the opposite direction go back over and under opposite your first line of weaving. That is, go under the warp you went over previously and over the warp you went under. (Figure 22.)

Weave somewhat loosely but, at the end of each row, use your fork to pack the thread tightly by beating it toward the pins at the top. Don't pull your weaving thread too tightly because it will distort the outer warp threads, and pull them toward the center. You are filling in space with thread and weaving a shape in color to match your pattern. (Photo 107.)

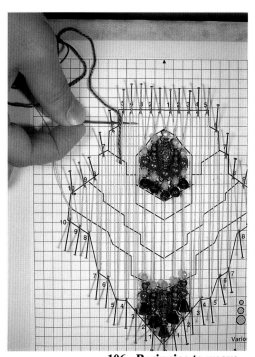

106. Beginning to weave. Lay the tail of your weaving thread along the outermost warp at the top. Then weave over and under across the warp and back again. When you come to the tail of your weaving thread, go around it just as if it were a warp thread.

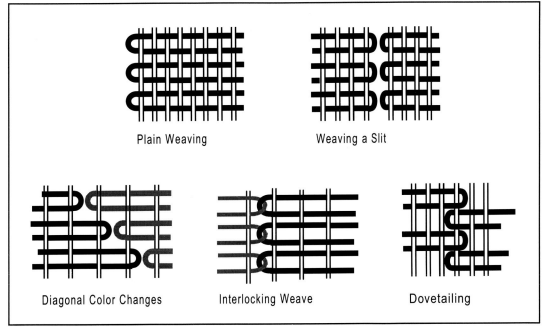

Plain Weaving   Weaving a Slit

Diagonal Color Changes   Interlocking Weave   Dovetailing

Figure 22. Weaving technique and various methods of making color changes

If you find that you are weaving too tightly or too loosely, try this: after you have brought your thread across a row of weaving, position it at a diagonal away from the woven edge. Then, beginning at the angle you have formed, use your fork to pack the thread firmly into place. The diagonal line of thread, when it is brought into place, will be exactly the right length and will not distort your necklace.

When you come to the slip knot in the warp thread on either side of the piece, pass the weaving thread through the loop of the knot at least twice. Also weave the warp tail into the piece by covering it with weft threads.

Weaving A Shape

Your pattern will indicate what shapes to weave. To weave the shapes, begin at the top, follow your pattern and weave over and under as many warp threads as needed to fill in the area.

In weaving a symmetrical design, I use two threaded needles and work alternately on each side of the piece in order to keep track of the area of each color and make each area the same size and shape. This also provides a better view of the finished part compared to the total composition.

A slit in the weaving is created wherever the beads are placed on the warp. This creates an open lacy effect as in a kilim rug.

- Helen Banes

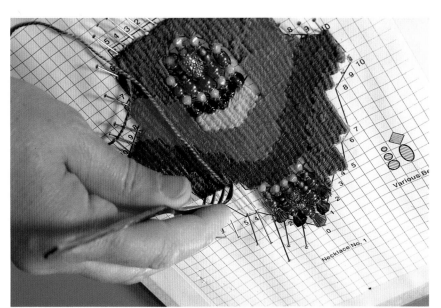

107. Continually pack your weaving thread toward the top pins. It must be closely packed to completely cover the warp.

Changing Colors Or Adding New Thread

To add a new thread or color, first weave the end of the old thread back through three to four previous rows by passing the needle vertically along a warp thread. Cut your old thread off where it comes out of the woven section. Next, thread your needle with a new thread. Just to the side where you wish to begin weaving again, pass the needle through three to four rows of weaving. Leave a 1/2 inch tail to be clipped off later. (Photos 108 and 109.)

When the weaving is completed, clip any remaining ends, remove the pins and try your necklace on! If the threads are packed correctly, the necklace should not change shape. (Photo 110)

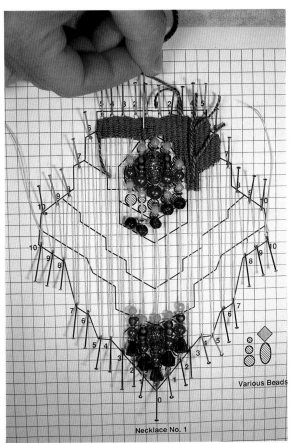

108. Bury the tail of your yarn by passing the threaded needle along a warp thread into the woven part.

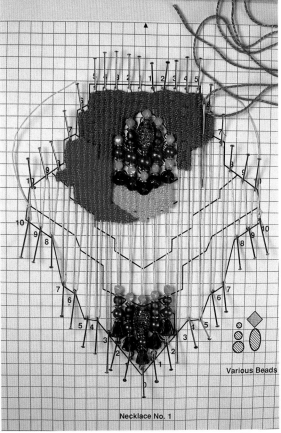

109. Begin a new thread by passing the needle along a warp and through 3 to 4 rows of a woven section. Be sure to continue the same over/under pattern of weaving.

110. The sample necklace completed with a four-strand braid as the support.

Finishing Your Necklace: The Support And Closure

The support and the closure are the parts of the necklace which allow it to hang around the neck. There are an endless variety of ways to create supports and closures and several possibilities are explained below. Since it is important that the support relate to the rest of the necklace, it is a good idea to reserve some beads and threads for this finishing. It is also a good idea to make the support in such a way that the length of the necklace is adjustable so that it can be worn with different garments. Here are some ways to make supports.

Support and Closure for Pendant Shapes:
(Necklace patterns Nos. 1, 2, 3 and 11 are pendant-shaped.)

There are many different ways that supports and closures can be added to your necklace. I have described five of them below.

1. You may attach your necklace to a metal neck ring or a chain by overcasting the two together with matching thread. First pass the needle between a pair of warp threads, then around the ring or chain, and then again through the next pair of warp threads. Alternatively, stitch the necklace onto a metal ring covered with tubular cord or wrapped with related threads.

2. String one or more strands of beads on your weft threads and attach these strands to your necklace. (Because your weft threads will probably be thicker than your warp threads, you may require beads with larger holes.) Braid the ends for an adjustable support. To attach the threads, pull them through the top of a warp pair with a crochet hook before braiding. You can make a three strand braid with six strands, by treating two strands as one.

3. Attach two or more strands of weft threads to your necklace by looping them around the warp threads at the edge of your necklace, pulling them through with a crochet hook. Braid these threads. Pin the ends of the warp threads to the board for tension. (See Figure 23.)

4. Attach a beaded woven support: To do so, string new warp threads of the desired length through the tops of warp pairs. String beads on these new warps and weave around the beads in a pattern which is in keeping with the rest of your necklace. (While weaving,

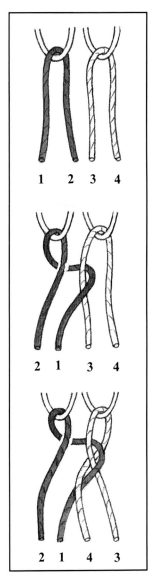

Figure 23. The Four-Strand Braid: A four-strand braid results in a round braid while a three-strand braid is flat. Loop two lengths of braiding thread through one or two warp threads at the top of your necklace. Then, with the four strands spread out before you as shown, number the strands 1, 2, 3, and 4. Pass #1 under #2 and #3 and back over #3. Then pass #4 under the #1 and #3 and back over #1. Keep your tension firm as you braid.

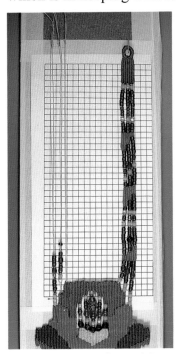

111. Warp extensions with beads.

112. Completed sample necklace with beaded and woven warp extensions.

tie the ends of the warps in a loose knot and secure to the board with a pin.) Finish the ends by wrapping. Add a loop to one end and a bead or button to the other end. (photos 111 and 112) see also Option 2 below in "Supports and Closures for Pieces with Curved Necklines."

5. Weave a slit about 3/4" long on each side of your necklace, near the top. Pass several threads through the first slit, continue on the back of the necklace, then bring them to the front again through the other slit. Wrap the ends to the threads to secure them. On one end, make a loop and on the other end make a knot or add a button to fit in the loop like a button and buttonhole. (Photo 113.)

Supports and Closures for Pieces with Curved Necklines

1. Necklaces with curved necklines usually have tabs that extend upwards from the body of the necklace. (See Pattern Nos. 12, 13, and 14.) These tabs may be woven with a vertical slit near the top or with a loop across the top of the tab. Attach grosgrain ribbon, braided or loose weft thread, chain or strands of beads to the slit or tab.

2. The tabs may also be extended by adding warp and continuing to weave. These extended tabs may be closed with snaps, hook and eye, Velcro, button and button hole, a ribbon tie or other jewelry fasteners.

To add warp, either as an extension of the tab or on the side of a pendant, use a crochet hook or needle to slip a strand of warp thread (about 24 inches or desired length) through the top of a pair of warp threads on the existing weaving. Bring the ends of the strand together to create a 12-inch pair of warps. Add as many warp threads in this manner as desired. Pin the new warps to the board where they join the old warps. Add beads as desired to cover the transition between warps by slipping the beads onto the warp pairs. By repeating the groupings of beads similar to those in the body of the piece, the extensions will create a continuous design. The amount of beads can vary from a single bead to the complete covering of warp threads with beads.

To add needleweaving to the extensions, pull the pairs of warps together into a loose, temporary, overhand knot. Pin this knot to the board to create tension for weaving. With a temporary knot, beads can be added after weaving, then more weaving can be added until the desired length is achieved.

At the end of the extension, form a loop, either horizontally or vertically, with the remaining warps and wrap them tightly, completely covering them. One option is to add a button or bead at one side and loop at the other. A second option is to make loops on both sides and weave a short piece with a button on both ends to attach to

113. Several strands of loose weaving thread can be used to create a support. Weave slits into the body of the necklace and finish the ends by wrapping.

the loops, somewhat like a long cuff link.

3. Weave a completely separate support using the same method as weaving the necklace. Attach it with buttons to slits woven in the tabs at the top of the necklace. (Photo 114.)

4. Wrap a double length of 1/8" to 1/4" diameter cord (sold in fabric stores to make piping) with weaving thread. Pin a loop of cord to a board of the desired length, then weave back and forth just like weaving around two warp threads (over and under and back over and under), covering the cord with thread. Attach buttons on the ends. (Photos 115 and 116.)

114. A necklace with a separate woven support with buttons. Slits are woven into the tabs to serve as buttonholes.

The most common query asked by people watching the process is, "How long does it take to make a necklace?" My response varies from, "As long as necessary," to "A very long time - but the result is worth waiting for," to "I lose all track of time while creating it."

- Helen Banes

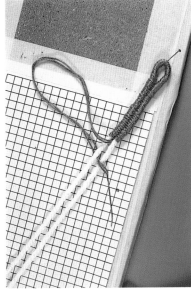

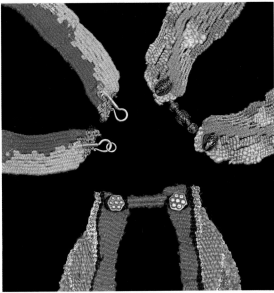

115. Making a wrapped support: This type of closure can be made in any length, with either buttons or loops at the ends. Sew the ends of a cord of desired length together to make a loop; pin the loop to a board so that it is stretched out as shown in the photo. Weave over and under the loop cords with weft thread until those cords are completely covered. You are wrapping the cord in a figure-eight fashion.

116. Various adjustable closures with buttons and hooks.

There are still new horizons to explore in needlewoven jewelry. Don't limit yourself to what's shown here. Perhaps you can create your own completely new technique! (Photos 117 to 120.)

117. Don't be afraid to explore new techniques as Susan Ramseier Paepcke did. Here, two pieces are woven separately and combined into one piece, stitched together across the top.

118. Susan's finished necklace.

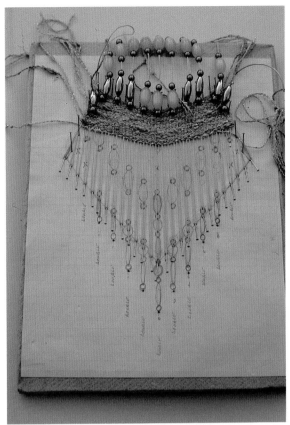

119. In this piece, Susan used a double set of warps. One set served as the woven background and the second set carried the beads. Above and below the beads both sets of warps were treated as one and woven together.

120. Susan's finished piece.

121. *Regina* **by Eugenia Nowlin.**

Patterns

On the following pages, you will see necklace patterns that range from the simple for beginners, to the complex for the more adventuresome. Some designs incorporate motifs from other periods or cultures and beads or artifacts related to these would enhance the design. Some designs can be used with ethnic or elegant beads. Depending upon your own personal style and the beads you have available, you may want to modify a pattern or create one of your own.

You have permission to make copies of the following 19 patterns for your personal use only and not for resale. Most of the patterns are shown full size; the others may be redrawn on a 1/4" grid or taken to your local copy shop, library, or other shop which has an enlarging copying machine to enlarge the designs to the size indicated.

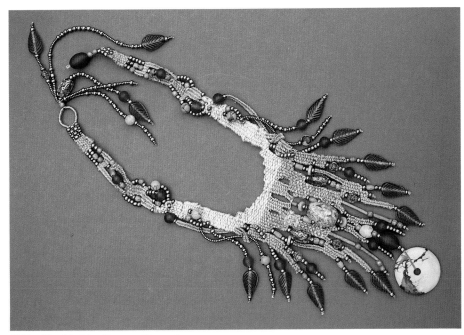

122. *Untitled* **by Laura Barnaby**

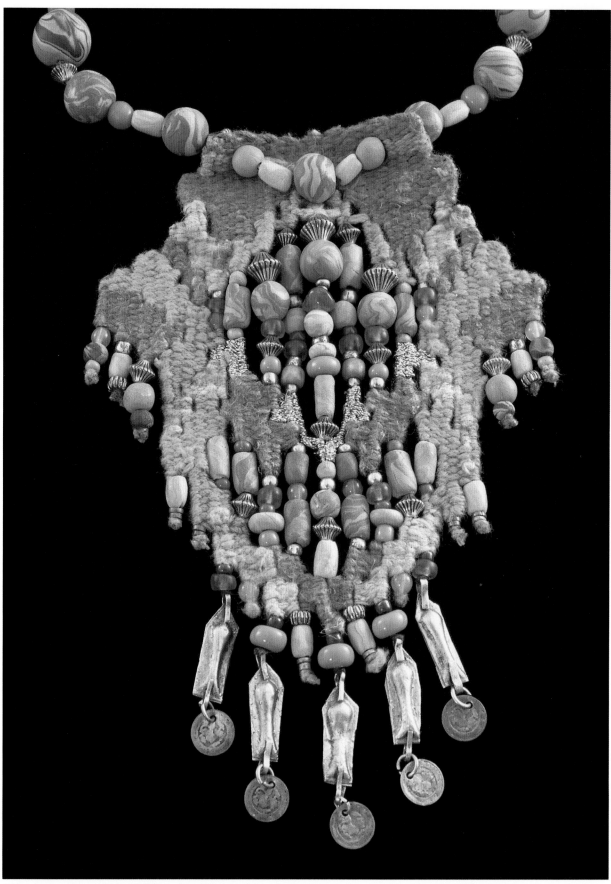

123.   A simple pendant necklace. See Chapter 3 for supports and closures. Necklace by Helen Banes.

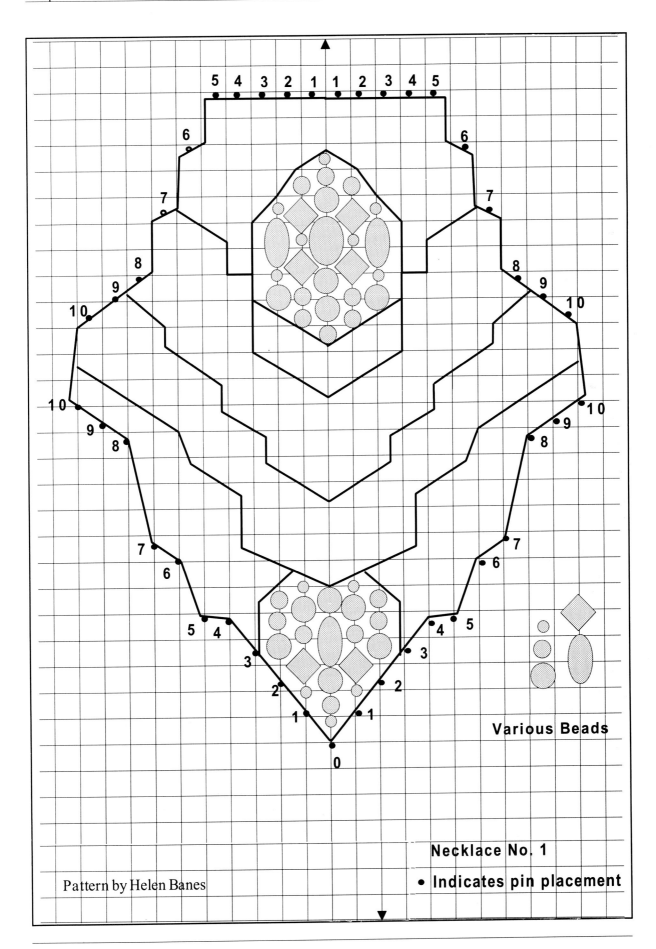

Various Beads

Necklace No. 1

• Indicates pin placement

Pattern by Helen Banes

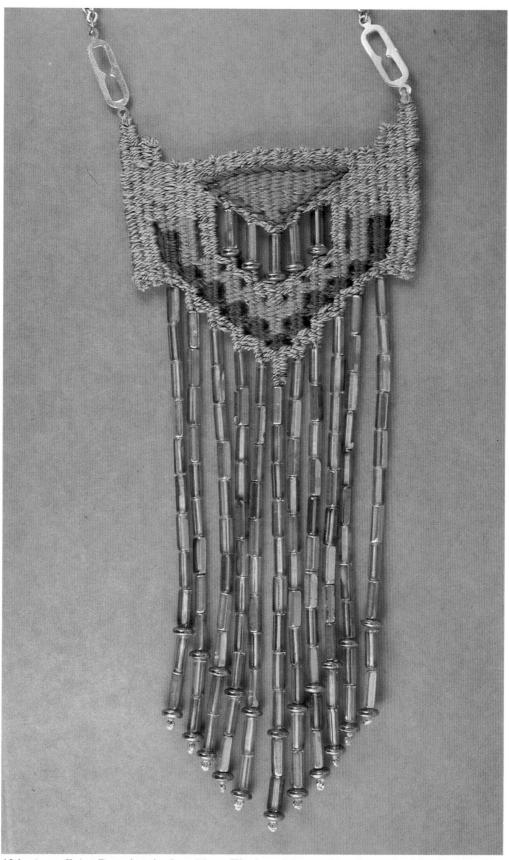

124. A small Art Deco-inspired necklace. The long fringes of beads require identical beads to continue this motif, but the pattern could be changed by using an assortment of beads. Necklace by Diane Fitzgerald.

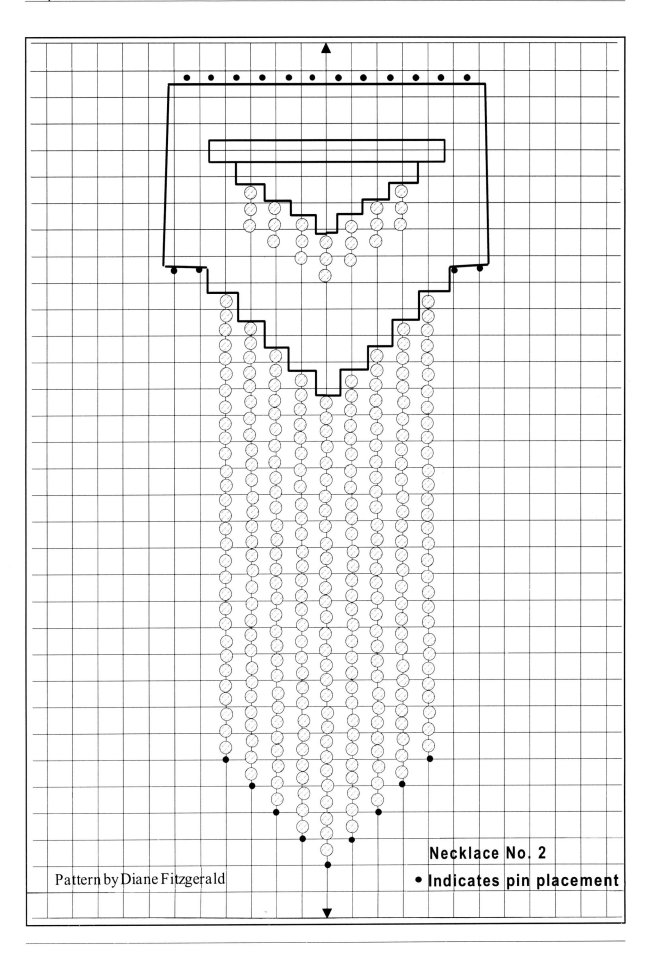

Necklace No. 2

Pattern by Diane Fitzgerald

• Indicates pin placement

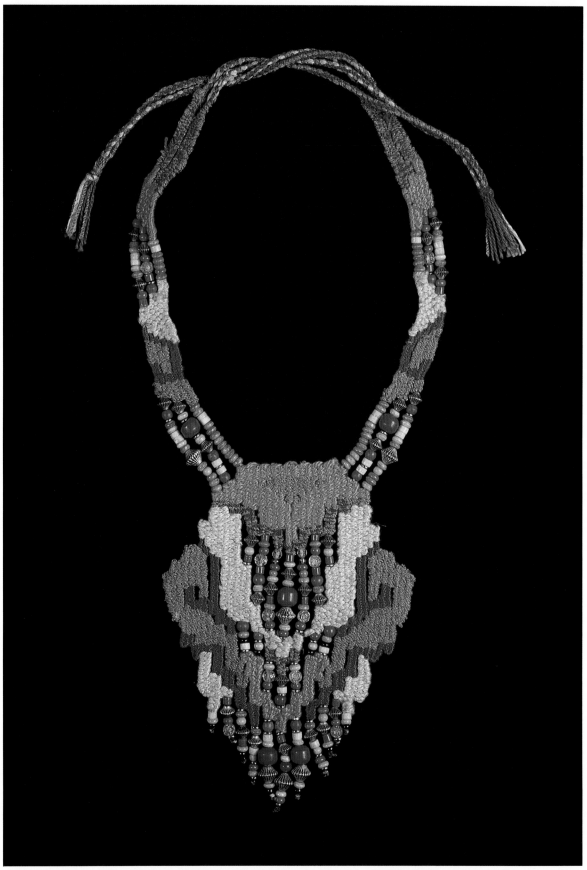

**125. Pendant necklace. Arrange light, medium and dark colors to emphasize the various shapes.
The support is woven with tie ends to allow adjustable length. Necklace by Helen Banes.**

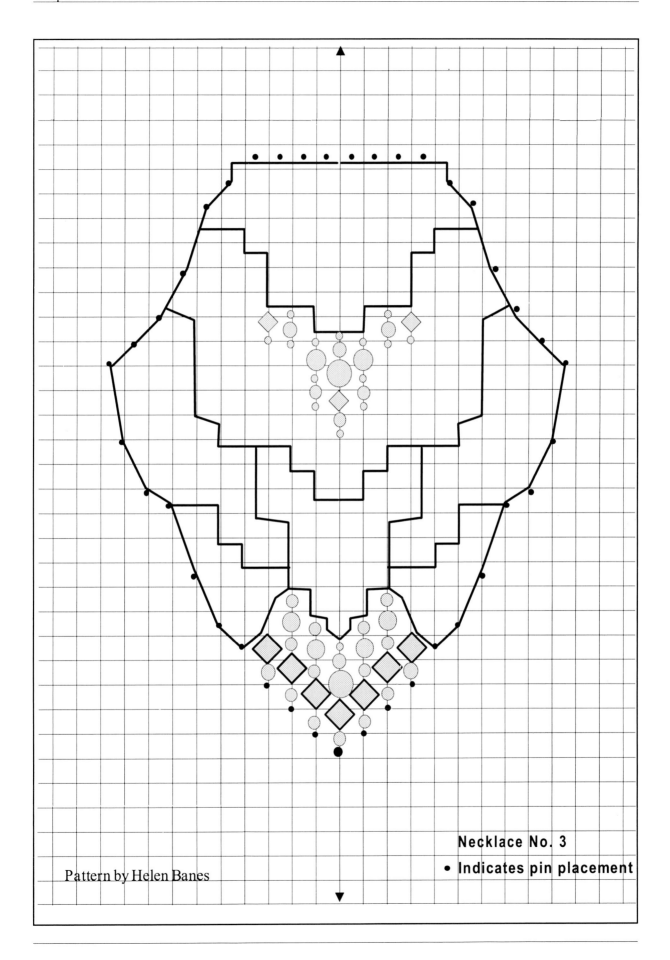

Necklace No. 3
• Indicates pin placement

Pattern by Helen Banes

126. A simple but elegant design woven in a single color. The beads will define the style. The sample, "Tuxedo," is woven with black thread to set off the luxurious crystal beads. After the weaving was complete, a bit of silver chain was added below the center beads after the weaving to give sparkle and movement. A silver chain is used for the support. Necklace by Diane Fitzgerald.

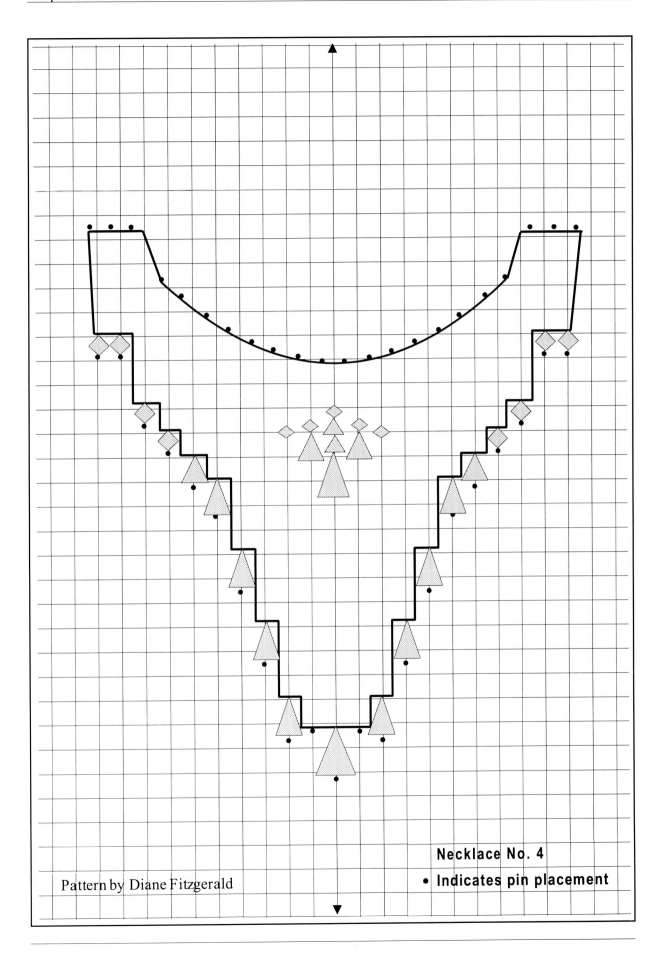

Necklace No. 4

• Indicates pin placement

Pattern by Diane Fitzgerald

127. Still in the "easy category," this necklace is similar to the pendant necklaces but has tabs at the top to which supports, such as braids, strands of beads, or wrapped strands, will be added. Closures are attached to the ends of these supports. The woven supports on the sample were added after completing the bottom portion. Necklace by Helen Banes.

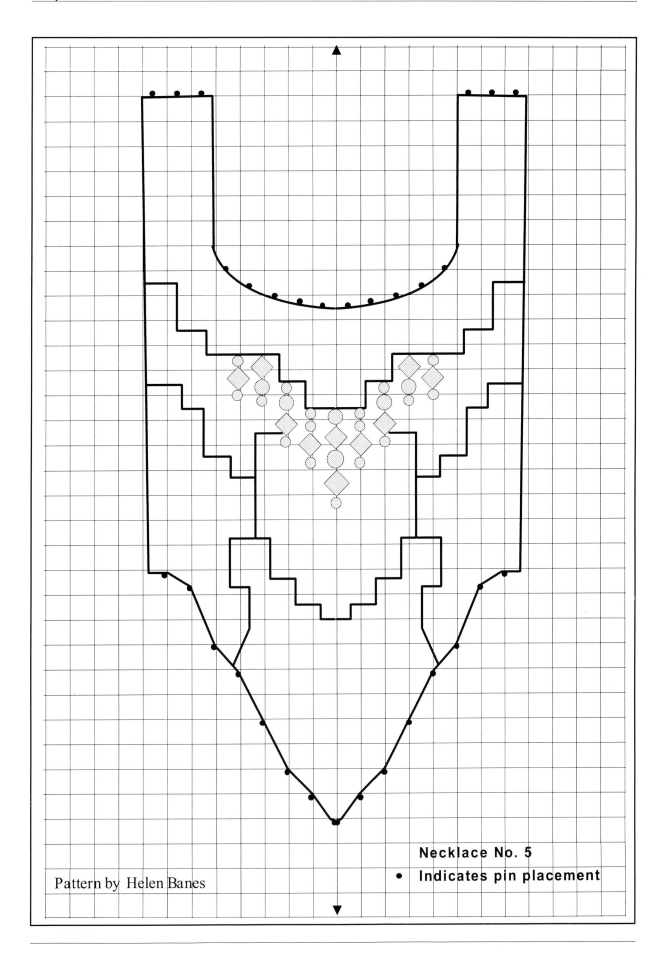

Necklace No. 5

● **Indicates pin placement**

Pattern by Helen Banes

128. An African-inspired necklace with a shallow curved neckline and a simple braided closure. Note that beads at the top, which begin to form the closure, are added from the top of the warp pair, rather than from the bottom. Beads used are light weight bamboo tubes and other wooden beads. Necklace by Diane Fitzgerald.

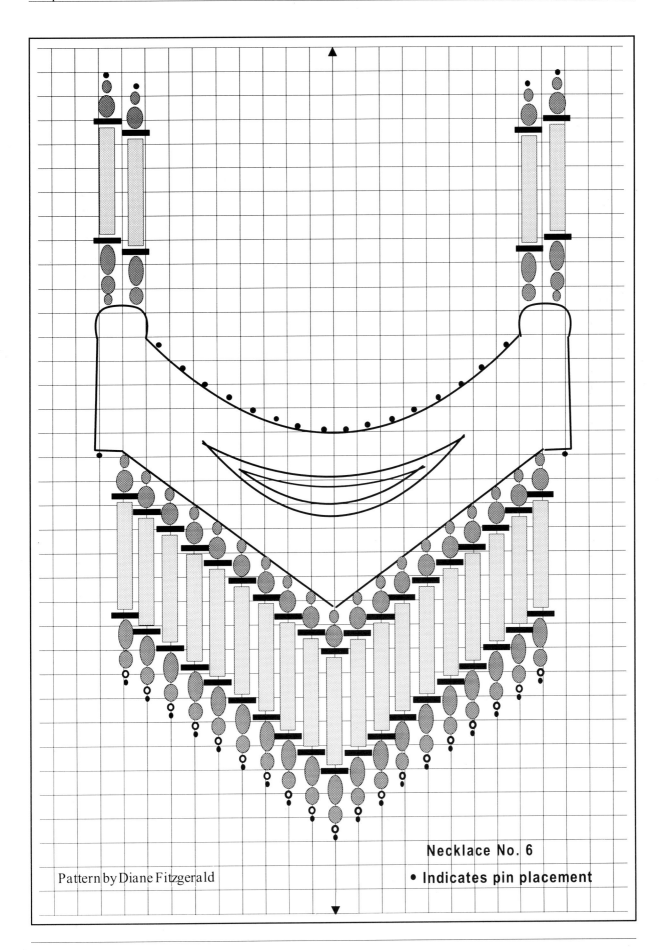

Necklace No. 6

Pattern by Diane Fitzgerald

• Indicates pin placement

129. Although crystal beads and pastel colors were used in the sample, ethnic beads and bright or dull colors would work equally well in this design. Necklace by Diane Fitzgerald.

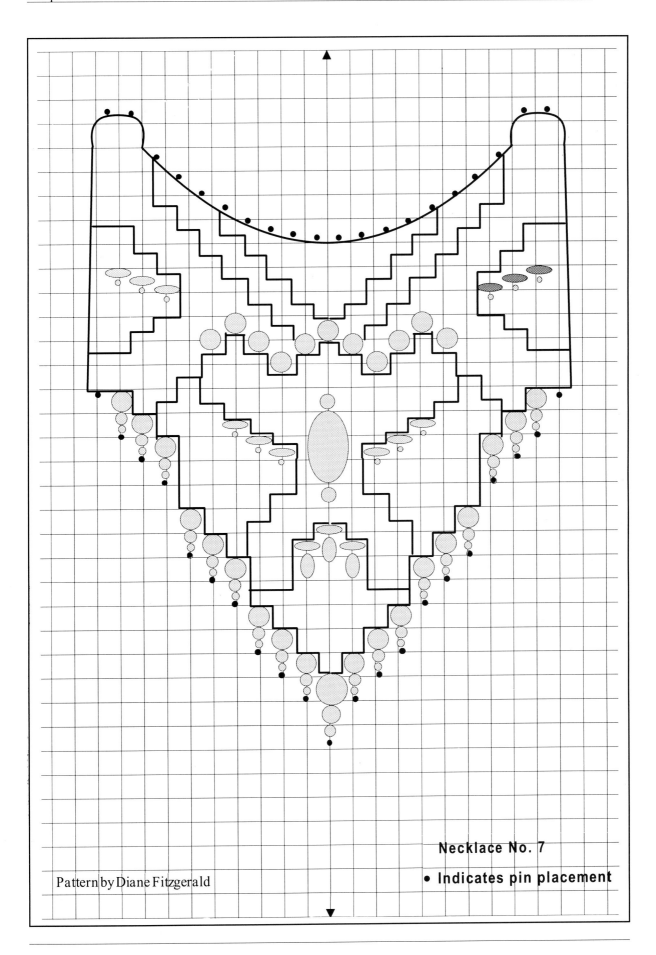

Necklace No. 7

• **Indicates pin placement**

Pattern by Diane Fitzgerald

130. *Peony Pink.* **Note the Oriental motif at the upper part of this necklace and in the tubular beads. The support can be braided strands of needleweaving (as shown) or wrapped fibers, or strands of beads. Necklace by Helen Banes.**

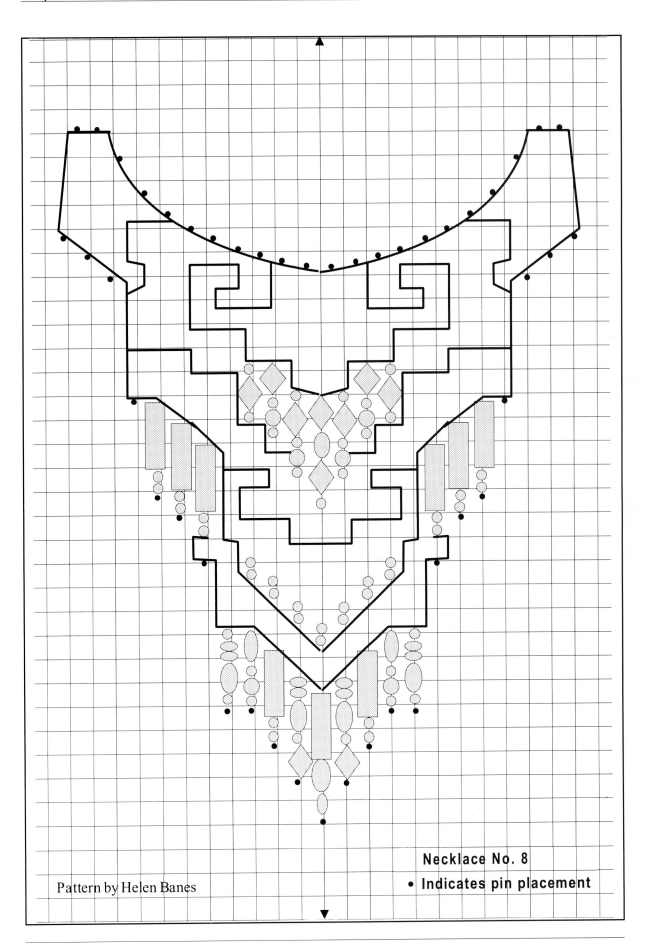

Necklace No. 8

• **Indicates pin placement**

Pattern by Helen Banes

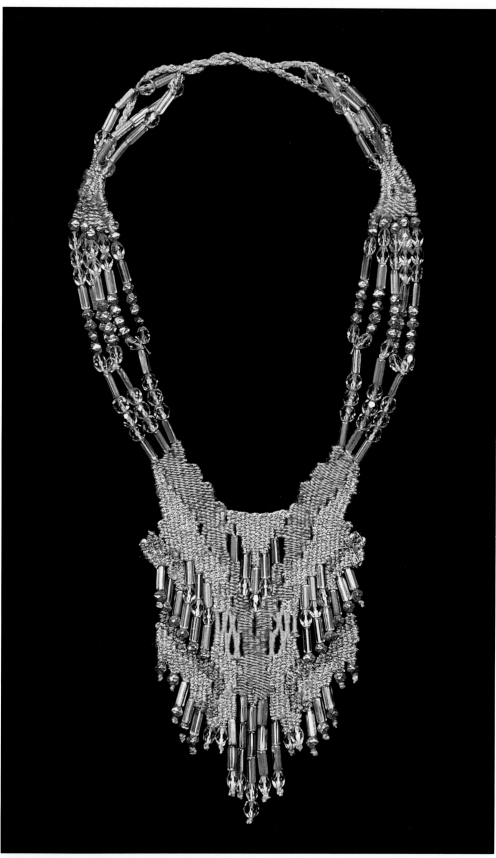

131. *Isadora*, another Art Deco-inspired design with many six-sided tubular and faceted beads in both the pendant and the support. Note that the pattern for this necklace is drawn on 5 to the inch graph paper. Necklace by Helen Banes.

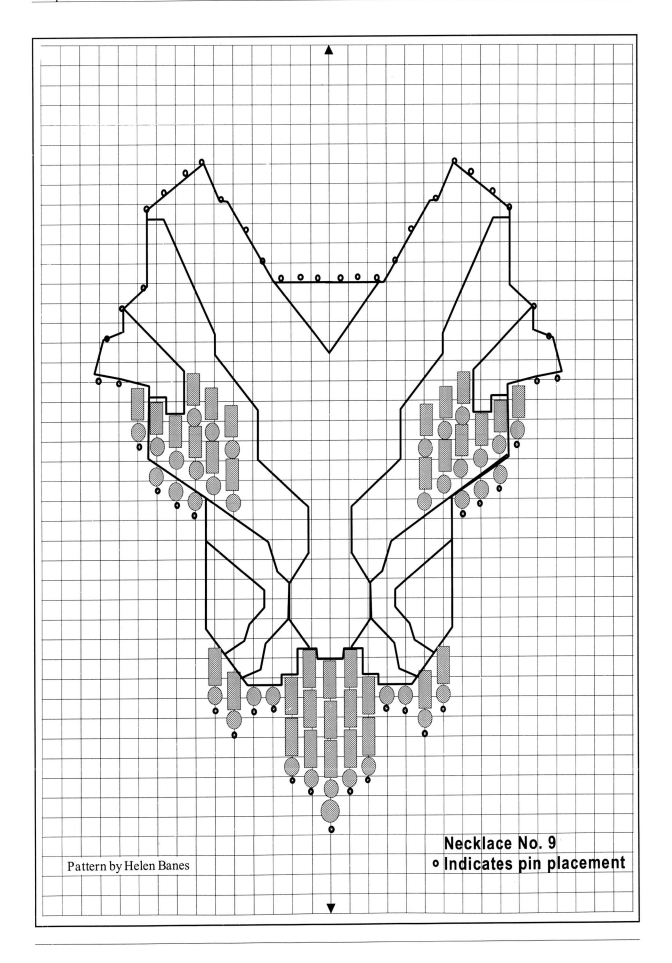

Pattern by Helen Banes

Necklace No. 9
○ **Indicates pin placement**

132. For quilt-lovers, this nine-patch interpretation is simple to do—lots of weaving but few beads. Necklace by Helen Banes.

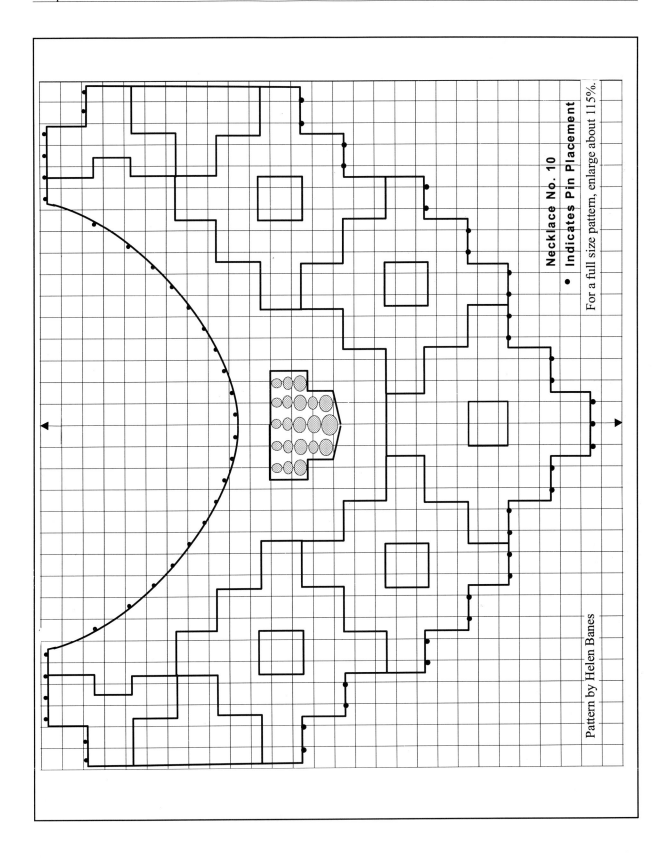

Necklace No. 10

• **Indicates Pin Placement**

For a full size pattern, enlarge about 115%.

Pattern by Helen Banes

133. *Navaho Spirit.* **This Navajo-inspired piece requires many, many beads. Instead of beads in the center, it could be woven solid so that a pin or pendant could be attached. Necklace by Helen Banes.**

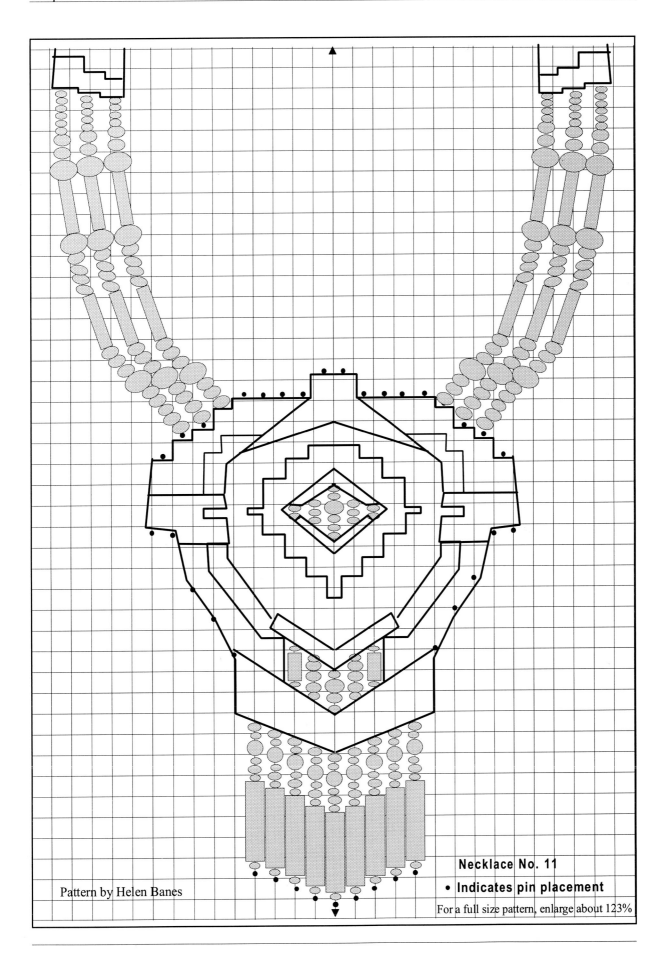

Pattern by Helen Banes

Necklace No. 11

• Indicates pin placement

For a full size pattern, enlarge about 123%

134. Color choice and bead selection will determine the overall character of this versatile pattern. Necklace by Helen Banes.

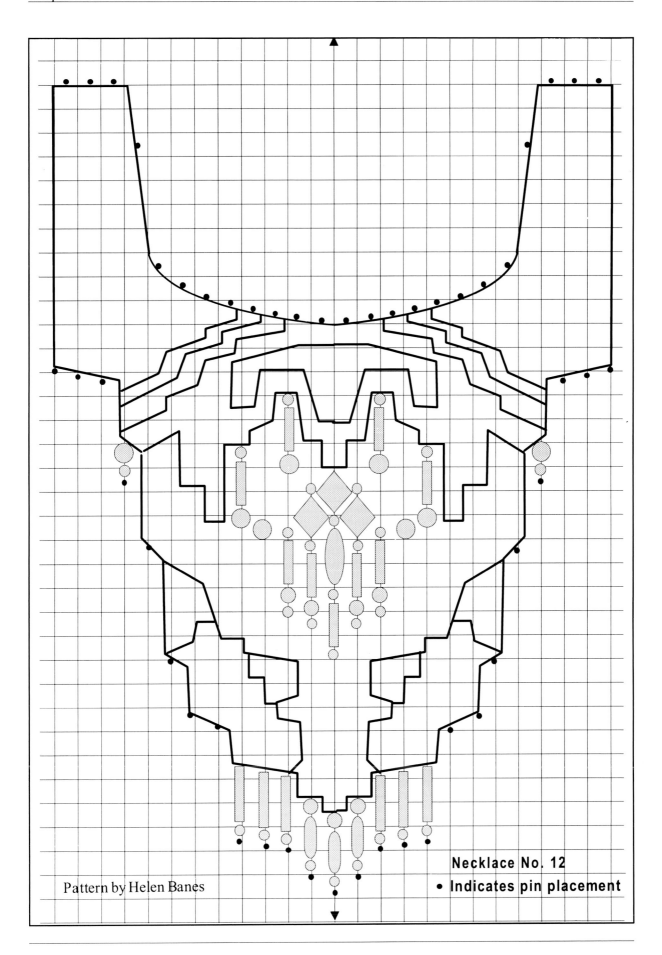

Pattern by Helen Banes

Necklace No. 12

• Indicates pin placement

135. *Untitled.* **A larger necklace for those who like to weave. The layering effect of the design could be executed in bright, medium and dark colors. Necklace by Diane Fitzgerald.**

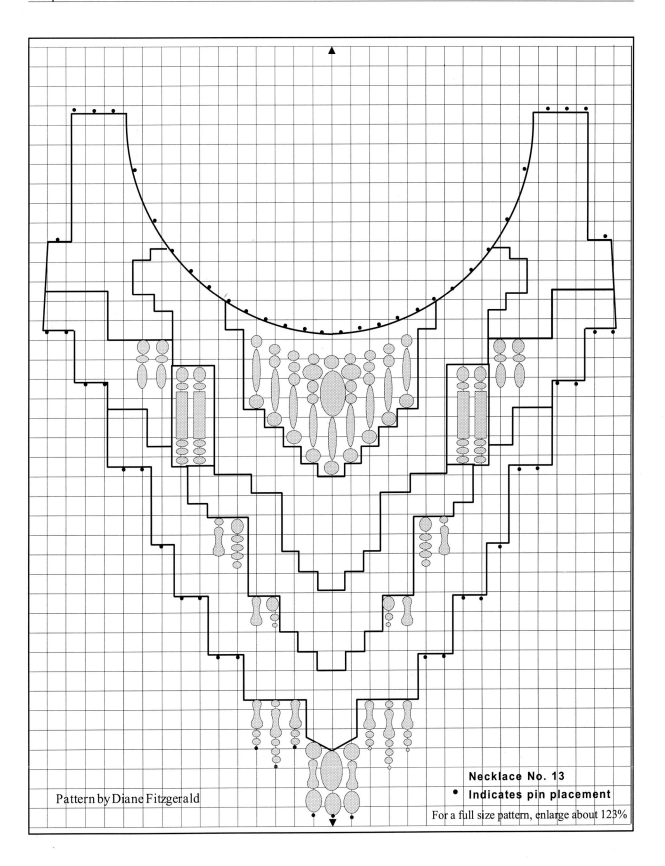

Necklace No. 13
● Indicates pin placement

Pattern by Diane Fitzgerald

For a full size pattern, enlarge about 123%

136. *Royal Pectoral.* **This bold pattern is somewhat more complex and does not require beads. The strong geometric pattern is shown to advantage with the striking colors used in the sample. Necklace by Helen Banes.**

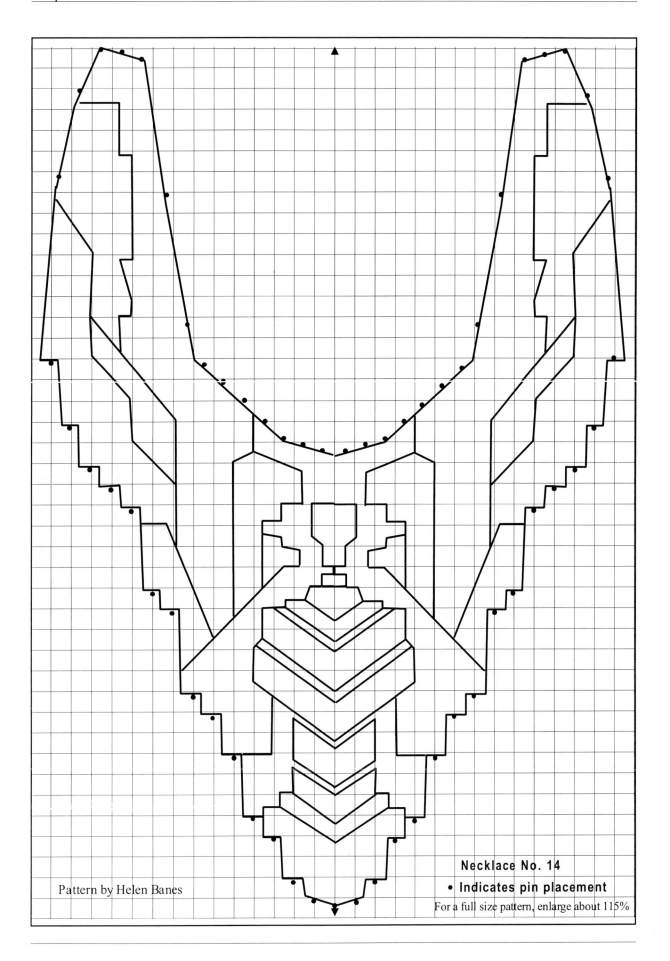

Pattern by Helen Banes

Necklace No. 14
• **Indicates pin placement**
For a full size pattern, enlarge about 115%

137. This necklace with its bold geometric motif was made to go with a jacket designed by Marian Gartler, using an African strip weave woven in hot magenta, yellow and green. Note that the extensions for the top tabs of the necklace must be added when redrawing the pattern. Match the arrows at "A" on the tab to the arrows marked "A" on the necklace. Necklace by Helen Banes.

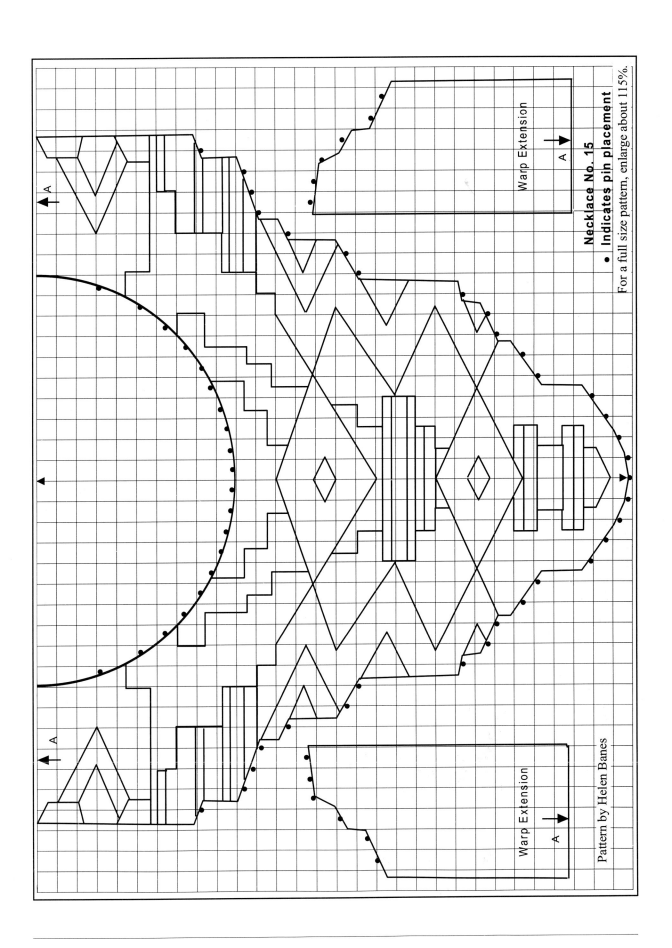

Necklace No. 15
● **Indicates pin placement**

For a full size pattern, enlarge about 115%.

Warp Extension

Pattern by Helen Banes

138. This asymmetrical design, "Black Diagonal," was inspired by and woven to complement a striped jacket created by Tim Harding in his "slashed fabric" technique. Note that the striped beads from Lebanon carry out the striped theme. Necklace by Helen Banes.

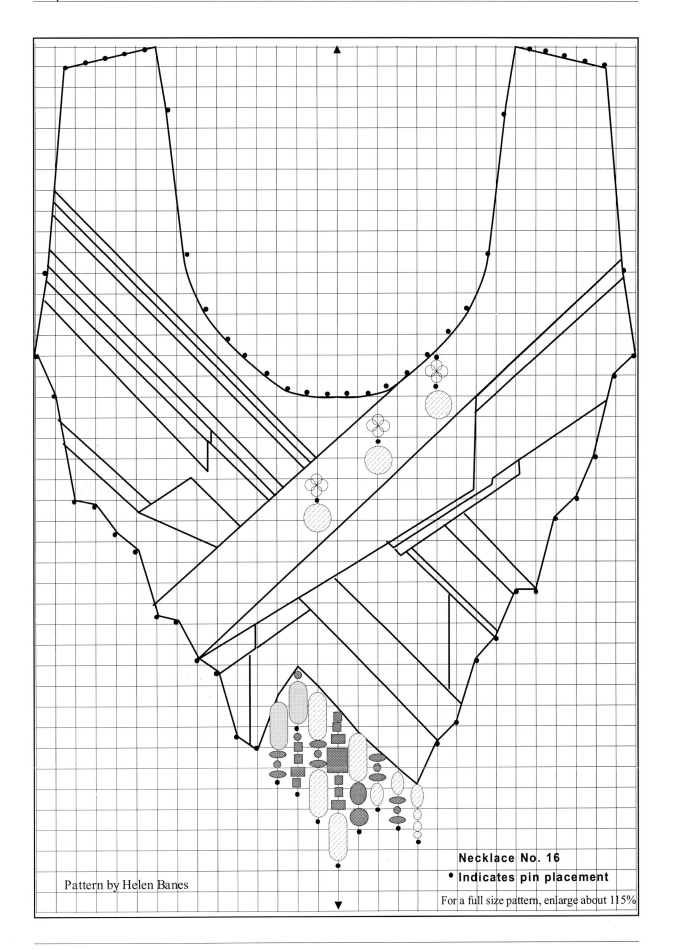

Necklace No. 16
• Indicates pin placement
For a full size pattern, enlarge about 115%

Pattern by Helen Banes

139. *Thunderbird.* **The center shape is left plain so that a pin or pendant can be added at that point. Necklace by Helen Banes.**

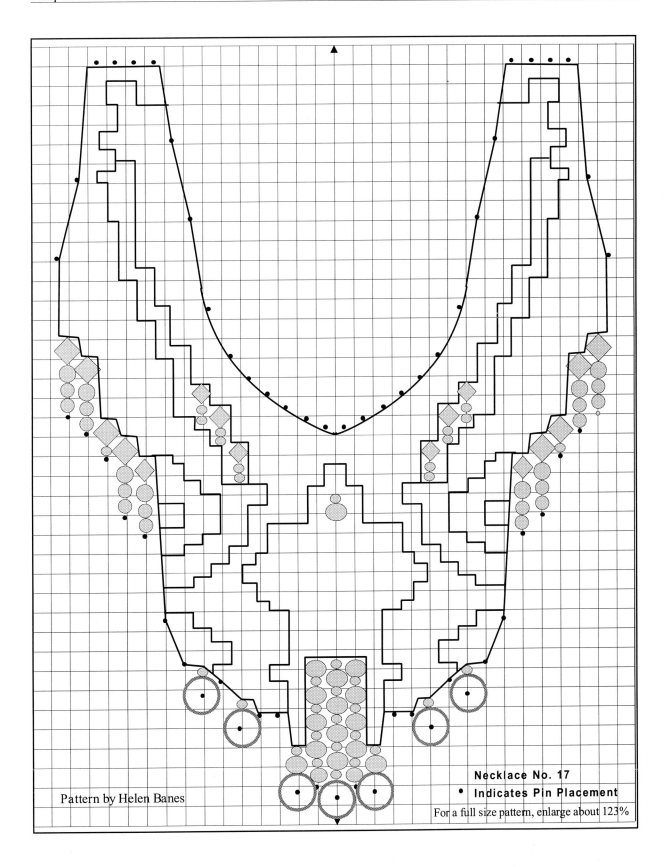

Pattern by Helen Banes

Necklace No. 17
• Indicates Pin Placement
For a full size pattern, enlarge about 123%

140. *Le Grande Kabyle (Detail).* This necklace tapers to a V-shape and a pendant and more beads could be added at the center of the V. Photo 1 on page iv shows the complete necklace. Necklace by Helen Banes.

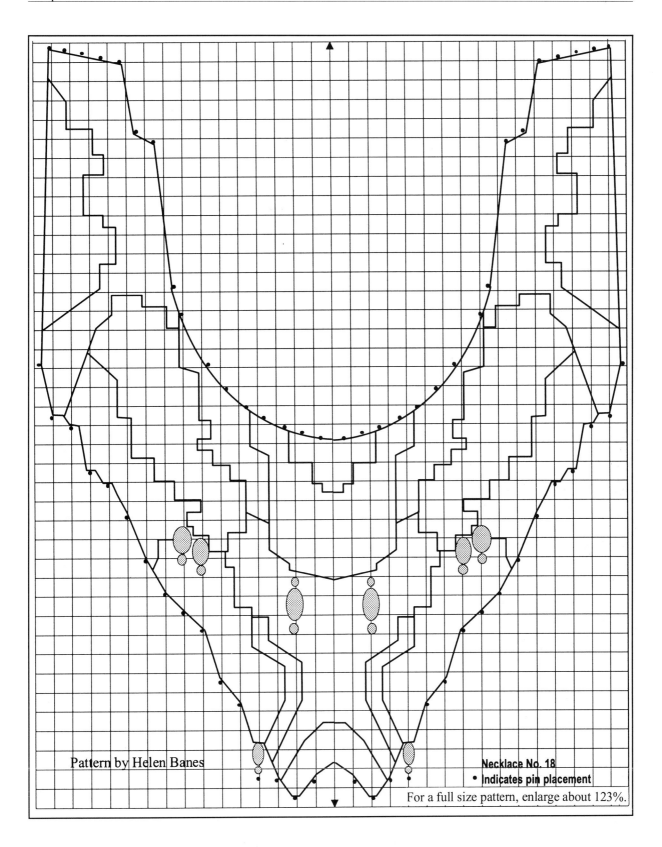

Pattern by Helen Banes

Necklace No. 18
• Indicates pin placement
For a full size pattern, enlarge about 123%.

141. *Cloud Collar for Jadine.* For this pattern, some warp threads are strung vertically and others are strung horizontally. With this warping method, a more smoothly curved outer edge may be achieved. (See also photo 142, page 112.) Necklace by Helen Banes.

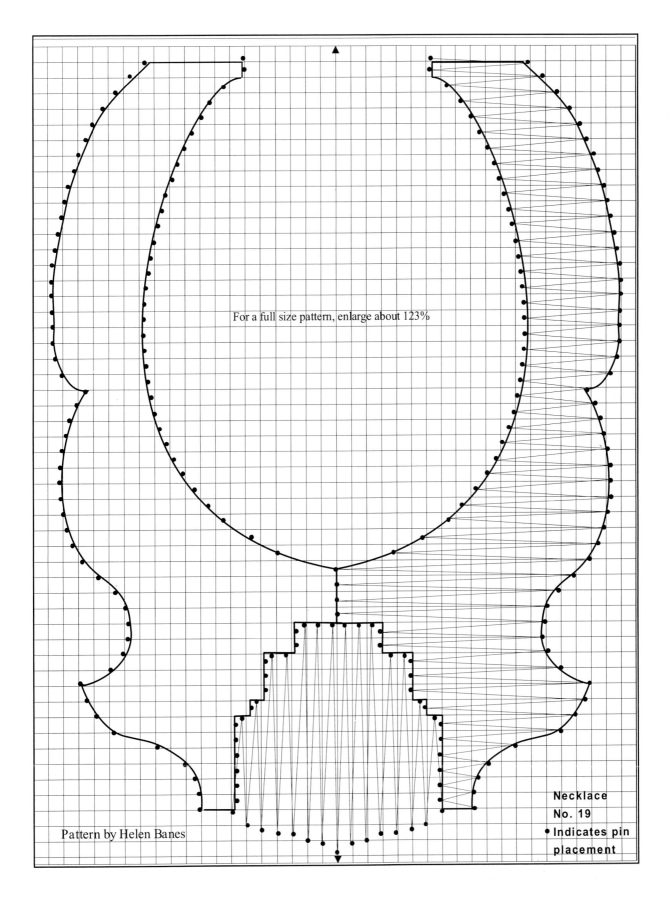

For a full size pattern, enlarge about 123%

Pattern by Helen Banes

Necklace
No. 19
• Indicates pin
placement

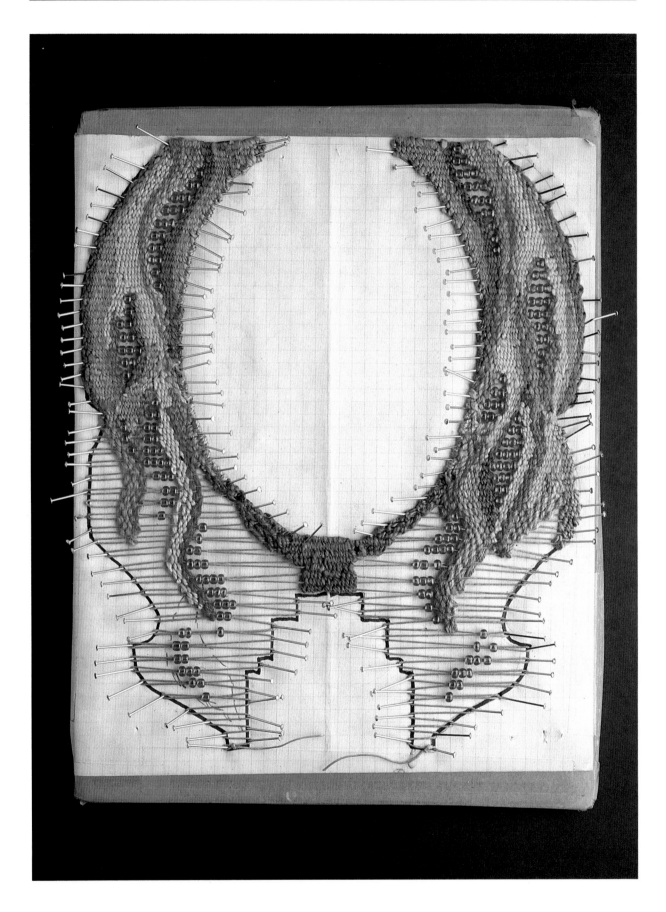

142.   Work in progress. Necklace by Helen Banes.

Finding or Making the Perfect Beads for Your Necklace

Why are we so fascinated with beads? For me, beads are miniature works of art, expressions of creativity, or sculptures. With beads, you can have an entire gallery on a simple string ready for your eye to behold at any time. They may seem to command far more attention than they deserve, yet we love to hold them and look at them, to say nothing of wearing them. Beads can symbolize status, accomplishment (such as the wooden beads awarded to Campfire Girls), wealth, affection, or beliefs.

143. An assortment of beads from around the world.

The Hunt For Beads

How do you find the perfect beads for your necklace? One way is to decide in advance exactly what kind of beads you want and to limit your search to those special beads. You don't accumulate a lot of beads that way and won't be troubled with a storage problem. The disadvantage? It's not much fun.

True bead lovers take another approach. They buy any beads which appeal to them, as many as they can afford, recognizing that they may never see those exact beads again. Although they may not have a specific use for a certain bead right now, they're thinking to the future, buying what they like and knowing that eventually the beads will work for some future project or perhaps will be traded for other beads later on. (Photo 143.)

I think of this as the more "painterly approach." Like a painter, a bead artist creates new adornments using a selection of colors, shapes and styles. While painters have merely to buy a range of oil, acrylic or water colors, then mix only the desired color on their palette and paint shapes as needed, bead artists must accept the shapes and colors of beads already set when we buy them. It's nearly impossible to change the shape of a bead, and changing its color is equally difficult. Only if you make your own beads from raw materials can you control the color and shape of a bead.

144. A "find" from an antique shop in London: a set of three ojime, carved Japanese beads, which portray the three monkeys who hear no evil, see no evil and speak no evil.

A woman who stopped by my shop recently echoed this idea. She remarked how much easier her work is when she has a wide selection of colors and shapes from which to choose when she makes her bead and postage stamp collages. Another person who specializes in earrings takes a similar approach. "Assembling beads into earrings or bracelets is almost like putting together a jigsaw puzzle," she said. "With a variety of shapes and colors at your fingertips, you can create wonderfully new intricate shapes that intrigue the viewer and captivate the buyer."

Beads can turn up in the most unusual places. Some of the more obvious places to begin your hunt, of course, are bead shops. As the popularity of beads increases, so do the number of bead shops. There may be one near you.

Antique stores are another obvious place to look. Old beads can be cheap or pricey, but for the most part they will be different from those made today. New techniques for making beads have been developed and new materials are in use. (Photo 144.)

Gem and mineral dealers travel from city to city on a regular basis. Watch for their ads in major city newspapers. They, too, will have beads. Sometimes the holes in stone beads are a little smaller than in other beads. If you take a piece of warp thread along with you, you can check them out.

While you're bead hunting, don't overlook flea markets, thrift shops, charity shops, garage, tag and estate sales (referred to as "boot sales" in Great Britain) and odd little shops or boutiques that carry miscellaneous small items. A bead collector friend suggested to me that the best buys she has found are from antique dealers who specialize in items other than beads. These people may pick up beads along with their other purchases but may not wish to take time to research appropriate prices. Of course, variety stores and craft or hobby shops often carry a selection of the more common wooden, plastic or seed beads. In the Yellow Pages of your phone book, check the "Beads," "Jewelry," or "Craft Supplies" categories for names and locations of stores.

Because almost any perforated item, including electronic parts, metal washers, plastic connectors and the like, can be used as a bead in needlewoven jewelry, you may wish to check out hardware stores and electric or electronic suppliers. Another unlikely place where I've found delightful items is the fishing section of sporting goods stores!

Although beads are made in many countries around the world, the major sources of glass beads are Czechoslovakia, Germany, Japan, France, Korea, India and China.

Making beads can be very labor intensive; their cost varies with their place of origin and their intricacy. The prices of some expensive beads will seem less exorbitant when you understand how the beads are made and what it takes to get them to you.

Beads can turn up in other unexpected places. A hike along a seashore or river bed could yield a rare find, some natural treasure or bead that has been washed up on the beach and is just waiting for you to take your turn owning it. Once you let friends know you are hunting for beads, they may clean out a few treasures from their drawers and jewelry boxes for you.

If you want to learn more about beads, begin by reading, asking questions and visiting museums. You may like to volunteer to be part of an archeological team and dig for beads. (Although you probably won't be able to keep the beads you may find, you will learn a lot about ancient beads and their sources.)

Travel to foreign countries takes on a whole new dimension when beads become the primary or even secondary focus. Advance research is very helpful. Before I leave on a trip, I learn how to say "bead" in the language of the countries I will visit and read as much as I can about the beads available there. I check prices at home before I leave. Then, too, I take along a few beads to show what I am looking for and a booklet which describes the bead making process with pictures. You can check foreign Yellow Pages in some libraries for bead stores, but a local person might be more helpful and could make phone calls for you. In many countries, items like beads are sold in markets or bazaars. Take a casual stroll and look around carefully. As soon as you find one person who sells beads, you probably will have a link to a network of other bead sources. Then the fun begins.

When traveling be sure to take time to observe how people wear and use their beads for personal adornment, in their homes, to decorate animals or in other ways. Are their stringing techniques unusual? Do they apply them to clothing? What do the beads, their colors and shapes symbolize? Are the beads made locally or imported? Can you visit the manufacturing site? Take pictures if possible and share your adventure with other bead lovers when you return.

Bead societies have formed in many major cities across the country. These groups may host "Bead Bazaars" or "Bead Swaps" which

145. A triple-strand necklace with Peruvian spindle whorls. Designed by Helen Banes.

American
Bead

French
Perle

Italian
Perla

German
Glasperle

Polish
Paciorek

Czechoslovakian
Koraleky

offer an opportunity to acquire beads and to learn more about them. Making new friends with people who have a common interest in beads is a pleasant side benefit. A list of current bead societies is shown in the Appendix. Button collectors also have associations and offer exhibits and sales.

Perhaps the best way to learn about beads and bead sources is through books and magazines. Several are listed in the Bibliography. One of them, *Ornament*, is a wonderful quarterly magazine about beads, jewelry and wearable art. It focuses on human adornment and features the work of recognized and emerging artists.

In your search don't overlook buttons, pins, or even rings as possible parts of a future needlewoven necklace. Don't forget that items which are not beads can become beads in several ways. Drill a hole in the item, using a variable speed drill and a very fine bit. If it is plastic, you may be able to heat a nail or heavy needle and pierce it. You can also glue on a bail, a metal finding like a handle, often available in rock shops.

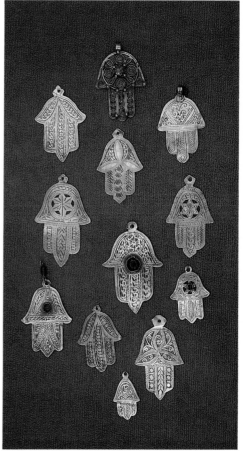

146. A collection of silver hand pendants from Morocco.

Bead Materials

Amber

Since it is fairly soft and easily bored, amber was one of the materials first used for beads. People have long believed that amber has mystical and curative powers. Its original source is the fossilized resin of pine trees which grew around the Baltic Sea. The color of amber can vary from golden yellow to a murky, reddish brown. It is highly prized if it naturally contains remnants of insects or parts of plants. Beware of fraud, though. Modern methods of making beads that resemble amber can be used to fuse an insect within the material.

Wound or Lamp Beads

"Wound" or "lamp" beads take their name from the technique by which they are made, lampworking. Working with a torch, molten glass is carefully wound around a thin metal rod, then shaped as the bead maker desires. Later, the bead is slipped off the rod or the rod is dissolved with acid. In the hands of the skilled bead makers, this labor-intensive process can result in wonderful beads, some of which are highly decorated.

Amulets, Talismans and Symbols

Amulet is derived from the Latin "amuletum," meaning an ornament, gem or symbol believed to protect the wearer against evil, disease or witchcraft or to aid in love or strength.

Talisman is derived from the Arabic "Tasasm," meaning charm. While amulets were meant to protect against evil powers, talismans were conceived as magic media capable of affecting the outer world and bringing good fortune.

Aventurine Beads

Adventurine glass beads contain flecks of sparkling coppery crystals within their depths. Also called goldstone in earlier times, these beads were valued because no one understood how to make them! Only by chance would a batch of glass result which contained these particles, much to the delight of the glass maker. With the knowledge of modern chemistry, the secret was eventually discovered and today we can enjoy these beads at moderate prices.

Jet

Jet is fossilized coal which is faceted or carved and polished. This fairly light weight, shiny black material was popularized by Queen Victoria mourning the death of Prince Albert. A well-dressed Victorian lady would wear garments covered with jet.

Coral

Coral is made of the skeletons of tiny sea creatures and is found in a range of colors. Deep-red coral is most valued, not only for its color, but because it is becoming more scarce. Like stone beads, its color may be enhanced with dye. Because it is easily pierced shortly after removal from water, early bead makers found this substance a delight to work with.

Wood

Wood beads are popular because they are relatively low-cost, can be painted or varnished in a wide variety of colors and are light-weight.

Caring For Beads

Most beads, new or old, will be dirty when you get them. Glass and plastic beads may be washed. To prevent breakage, place them on a cloth at the bottom of a non-metallic container. Soak them for a few minutes in a cup of warm water to which has been added two teaspoons of ammonia and a drop of a mild dishwashing detergent. (Close the stopper on your sink so the beads don't escape down the drain.) When they have finished soaking, swish them around, rinse them and lay them on a towel to dry. The washing will remove the accumulated dust and body oils from the beads and bring out their true colors.

Washing beads is easier if you leave the beads on the string. Be careful of the clasp when washing a string of beads. You may wish to remove it before washing beads. If rhinestones or other decorations are glued to the clasp, water may loosen them.

Other beads, such as stone, wood or ceramic beads, may be wiped with a damp cloth wrung out in warm soapy water. (Some stone beads are dyed and soaking could change their color.)

Symbols:

Hand: silver amulets worn in the Middle East, especially by the Muslims. The amuletic design of the hand, "Khamsa," literally means "five" and refers to the five fingers of the hand. It is also called the "Hand of Fatima," the favorite daughter of Mohammed. It is believed to provide protection from the "evil eye."

Crescent Moon: "Chand," the symbol of the Muslim faith

Fish: represents fecundity and fidelity

Sun Figure or Seeds: desire for fertility, the source of regeneration

Coins: symbols for wealth

Heart: desire for love and romance

Flowers or leaves: symbols of life and nature

Triangle: Hindu symbol for the female or fertility

Eye bead: any bead with an eye shape is believed to have the power to repel the evil eye of envy.

Turquoise and coral: Both these natural stones are regarded as protection in many cultures, especially by Tibetans, Native Americans and nomads of the Eurasian steppes.

Occasionally I have found crystal beads with extremely dirty holes. Sometimes these are almost impossible to clean, but there are several things you can try. I have soaked beads in "Lime Away," ammonia, laundry bleach, dishwasher detergent or white vinegar with varying degrees of success. Try threading a string through the hole and moving it back and forth to clean the holes. Dental bridge threaders work well for this, too.

Be careful not to drop beads on a hard surface. They can break!

Storing and Displaying Beads

Once you are hooked on collecting and maintaining your selection of beads for future necklaces, you'll need to store them so that you can find the specific beads you want when you want them. It can be very frustrating to know that you have the perfect bead, but can't find it. There's probably no ideal way to store beads and you'll probably find that you use a number of methods. Here are some that I've come across.

One friend separates beads by color and strings a sample of each of her beads with a small clear bead between each as a spacer. Not only does she add to the string as she gets new beads, but she can wear it as a necklace whenever she wants to. Another collector always buys one extra bead for her collection. She simply puts these extra beads in a large tin and takes them out occasionally to look at them. Others rely on the familiar clear plastic boxes with dividers which are available at variety, hardware and craft supply stores. Still others use those versatile and inexpensive self locking plastic bags. They come in a variety of sizes starting as small as one inch square. I prefer the plastic cabinets that hold from 9 to 60 small drawers. They take little space and offer convenient storage.

If you are really organized, you can sew sample beads on cards or tag board, give them numbers which are maintained in a card file or computer data base. Include bead type, color, material, cost, date acquired, storage location, other pertinent information and, if possible, a sketch.

Displaying beads in ways other than as jewelry can add considerably to your enjoyment of your beads. One collector has a display of two or three tiny baskets in which she places a few different beads to be admired each week. One could also place beads on the end of a wooden skewer, toothpick or thin metal rod then insert the other end in a cribbage board so that the beads stand up like lollipops. Some collectors string transparent beads and drape them across their windows or from lamp shades so the light passes through them. (Be aware that light, over a long period of time, can change the colors of some

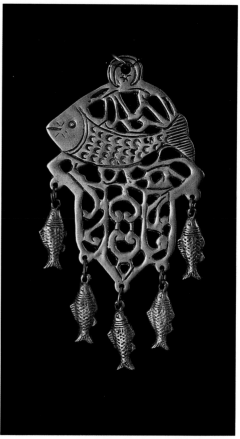

147. Hand and fish amulet from Israel attached to a wall or door.

glass.) I have used the plastic trays found in candy boxes as a holder for beads, then framed the tray in a metal shadow-box frame. Mug or cup hangers hung on the wall allow strings of beads or necklaces to be hung and admired. Decorate a small Christmas tree with your favorite beads. Why not go wild? Fill a wonderful crystal bowl with Swarovski crystal beads in all colors and sizes. I'm sure you'll think of other ways to store and enjoy your collection.

Making Beads

If you don't have a good bead store where you live, if you want to save money on beads, or if you simply want to try your hand at making unusual beads, you may want to try one of the following techniques. The materials are inexpensive and the process can be a lot of fun for adults and children.

Wound Paper Beads

This is perhaps one of the simplest ways to make beads. My mother, who grew up on a farm, told me that she and her sisters used to make beads this way using pages from old catalogs. Heavy paper, leather, or anything that can be cut and rolled, can be used. Simply cut a triangle with a 3/4" base and a height of 2-1/2 to 3" from your chosen material. For a thicker bead, use a longer triangle. For a thinner one, use a shorter triangle. The thickness of your material will also determine how thick your bead will be. Roll the triangle around a round toothpick or piece of heavy wire, such as a coat hanger, beginning with the widest end. Glue the tip of the triangle in place.

Shapes other than triangles can also be used and each results in a different bead shape. Always begin winding with the widest end. After the glue has dried, slip the bead off the toothpick and coat it with clear fingernail polish, clear plastic spray, varnish or other clear coating or dip the beads in pure candle wax.

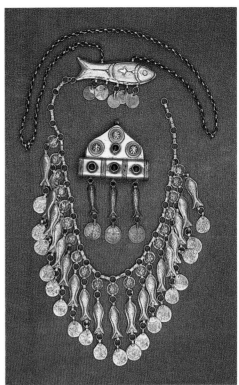

148. Fish and coin jewelry from the Bedouin tribes of Israel. Top: silver fish pendant with niello design, worn to insure fertility. Middle: amulet case with hollow section to hold inscription from the Koran. Bottom: Bedouin necklace with fish and coins.

Figure 24. Shapes for wound paper beads.

Several different shapes can be used. To embellish the beads further, try these ideas:

- Paint beads with watercolors, tempera paint or thick fabric paints.

- Wrap with thin wire, thread, yarn or other wrapping material and glue in place.

- Coat with glue or fingernail polish and roll them in glitter.

- Glue on dots, strips, stars or other shapes of contrasting paper or metallic paper.

- Attach feathers, sequins or bits of leather.

Dough Beads

2 cups of flour

1 cup of salt

1 cup of water

Mix the ingredients together and knead the mixture on a flour-covered board for a few minutes. Form into beads. (To make beads more uniform, roll the dough to a uniform 1/2" thickness, then cut into even squares.) Bake in the oven 1-1/2 hours at 250°. Paint with enamel, poster paints or water colors, then spray with clear acrylic varnish to seal the bead and give it a shiny finish.

149. Tibetan pendant with the Buddhist symbols of double fish and eternal knot, and coral and turquoise beads, two substances regarded as protection from illness.

Wire Beads

Wire comes in a variety of colors and thicknesses and for this reason works well for bead making. Plain, enameled or coated wire may be used. You should look for wire which is stiff enough to hold its shape well. Telephone cable is particularly fun to work with because it is possible to obtain cable with five to fifty multi-colored wires inside of it. Hardware and electronic stores are good sources of wire.

Cut the wire to the desired lengths for uniformity then wrap the wire around a toothpick, meat skewer, wooden bead or other item and tuck the ends into the center. Wrap two or more wires at the same time for a striped effect. Seed beads could be strung on the wire before it is wound to create other effects.

Wrapped Beads

Simple wooden beads can take on new elegance when wrapped with thread. Wrapping can coil around the outside of the bead perpendicular to the hole. Beads may also be wrapped by passing the thread through the hole again and again until the bead is covered. Glue ends with white glue.

Polymer Clay Beads

Polymer clay is a modeling compound which is easily shaped and baked in an oven. Although it was discovered early in this century in Germany, it has become popular in the United States only in the last five to ten years. The material comes in a wide variety of colors and can be mixed to make other colors. It is sold under such brand names as Fimo, Sculpey, Cernit and Modello. The clay must be kneaded to make it smooth and malleable. Some people use a pasta machine to do this. When the clay is workable, beads can be made using many of the old glass making techniques such as millefiori, and others. For further information on making beads with polymer clay, see "The New Clay," mentioned in the Books section. (See Photos 150-153.)

150. Fetish necklace with birds made in the style of the Navajo multi-strand necklaces. The bird fetishes and many of the beads are made of polymer clay as are the spacer bars at the shoulder line which keep the strands separate. Other beads are crystal and glass.

151. A scarab necklace by Helen Banes using mold making techniques. Also shown is a mold and the scarab that made it.

152. Egyptian-Style Scarab Necklace. The multiple elements are created by forming a mold from an original scarab which was pressed into a ball of polymer clay which was then baked to harden it. Duplicates of the original form can be made by pressing balls of clay into the mold. The new scarab is easily removed from the mold if both the mold and the clay are chilled. Created by Helen Banes.

"To tell one's beads" is a phrase reminiscent of the Middle English word for prayer, "bede," and marks another point in time when beads were symbolic of the spiritual aspect of people's lives.

- Diane Fitzgerald

153. Mermaid Pin with tabs to allow it to be attached to a needlewoven necklace. The pin can be worn separately. Designed by Kathleen Amt.

154. Art Nouveau Necklace by Helen Banes. Collection of Mary Alice Hearn.

Other Books and Publications

Books about Beads

Coles, Janet and Budwig, Robert. **The Book of Beads**. New York: Simon and Schuster, 1971.

Dieringer, Beverly. **The Paper Bead Book**. New York: David McKay, 1977.

Dubin, Lois Sherr. **The History of Beads**. New York: Harry N. Abrams, 1987.

Erikson, Joan Mowat. **The Universal Bead**. New York: W. W. Norton & Company, Inc., 1969.

Harris, Elizabeth. **A Bead Primer**. Prescott, AZ: The Bead Museum, 1987.

Jargstorf, Sibylle. **Glass in Jewelry: Hidden Artistry in Glass**. West Chester, PA: Schiffer Publishing, Ltd., 1991.

Mack, John, editor. **Ethnic Jewelry**. New York: Harry N. Abrams, 1988.

Millefiori Beads from the West African Trade, Volumes I - VI. Carmel, CA: Picard African Imports, (no date).

Poris, Ruth. **Advanced Beadwork**. Tampa, FL: Golden Hands Press, 1989.

Roche, Nan. **The New Clay**. Rockville, Maryland: Flower Valley Press, 1991.

Tomalin, Stefany. **Beads! Make Your Own Jewelry**. New York: Sterling Publishing, 1988.

van der Sleen, W. G. N. **A Handbook on Beads**. York, PA: George Shumway, Publisher, (no date).

Books about Design, Color or Design Inspiration

Color Sourcebook: **A Complete Guide to Using Color in Patterns** (Over 500 Patterns in Natural, Oriental and High-Tech Color Schemes) Rockport, MA: Rockport Publishers, 1989.

Cooper, J.C. **An Illustrated Encyclopedia of Traditional Symbols**. London: Thames and Hudson, 1978; reprinted 1990.

Evans, Helen Marie, and Dumesnil, Carla Davis. **An Invitation to Design**. New York: Macmillan Publishing Co., Inc., 1982.

Gillon Jr., Edmund V. **Geometric Design and Ornament**. New York: Dover Publications, Inc., 1969.

Haeckel, Ernst. **Art Forms in Nature**. New York: Dover Publications, Inc., 1974.

Kerimov, Lyatif. **Folk Designs from the Caucasus**. New York: Dover Publications, Inc.,1974.

Varley, Helen, Editor. **Color**. Marshall Editions Limited, 1980.

Walch, Margaret. **Color Source Book**. New York: Charles Scribner's Sons, 1979. (Presents and describes 48 historical to contemporary color palettes with color swatches.)

Wong, Wucius. **Principles of Color Design**. New York: Van Nostrand Reinhold, 1987.

Wong, Wucius. **Principles of Two-Dimensional Design**. New York: Van Nostrand Reinhold, 1972.

Wong, Wucius. **Principles of Three-Dimensional Design**. New York: Van Nostrand Reinhold, 1977.

Books on African Designs and Motifs

Beveridge, June, Editor. **Authentic Algerian Carpet Designs and Motifs**. New York: Dover Publications, Inc., 1978.

Fischer, Angela. **Africa Adorned**. New York: Harry N. Abrams Co., 1984.

Revault, Jacques. **Designs and Patterns from North African Carpets & Textiles**. New York: Dover Publications, Inc., 1973.

Williams, Geoffrey. **African Designs from Traditional Sources**. New York: Dover Publications, Inc., 1971.

Art Deco Designs and Motifs

Hillier, Bevis. **The World of Art Deco**. (Minneapolis Institute of Arts Exhibition Catalog.) New York: E.P. Dutton, 1971.

Deboni, Franco, Editor. **Authentic Art Deco Jewelry Designs**. New York: Dover Publications, Inc., 1982.

Fry, Charles Rahn. **Art Deco Designs in Color**. New York: Dover Publications, Inc., 1975.

Griffin, Leonard and Louis K. and Susan Pear Meisel. **Clarice Cliff: A Bizarre Affair**. New York: Harry N. Abrams, 1988.

Loeb, Marcia. **Art Deco Designs and Motifs**. New York: Dover Publications, Inc., 1972.

Menten, Theodore. **The Art Deco Style**. New York: Dover Publications, Inc., 1972.

Rowe, William. **Original Art Deco Designs**. New York: Dover Publications, Inc., 1971.

Weber, Eva. **Art Deco**. New York: Gallery Books, 1989.

Chinese Designs and Motifs

Full Color Designs from Chinese Opera Costumes. Dover Publications, Inc., 1980.

Mailey, Jean. **The Manchu Dragon: Costumes of the Ch'ing Dynasty**. New York: The Metropolitan Museum of Art, 1980.

Vollmer, John E. **In the Presence of the Dragon Throne**. Toronto: Royal Ontario Museum, 1977.

Vollmer, John E. **Five Colors of the Universe: Symbolism in Clothes and Fabrics of the Ch'ing Dynasty**. Edmonton, Alberta: Edmonton Art Gallery, 1980.

Egyptian Designs and Motifs

Andrews, Carol. **Ancient Egyptian Jewelry**. New York: Harry N. Abrams, 1990.

Wilson, Eva. **Ancient Egyptian Designs for Artists and Craftspeople**. New York: Dover Publications, Inc., 1986.

Native American Designs and Motifs

Branson, Oscar T. **Fetishes and Carvings of the Southwest**. Tuscon, AZ: Treasure Chest Publications, Inc.,1976.

Wilson, Eva, **North American Indian Designs for Artists and Craftspeople**. New York: Dover Publications, Inc., 1984.

Pre-Columbian Designs and Motifs

Anton, Ferdinand. **Ancient Peruvian Textiles**. London: Thames & Hudson Ltd., 1984.

Cahlander, Adele and Marjorie Cason. **The Art of Bolivian Highland Weaving**. New York: Watson-Guptil, 1976.

Cordry, Donald and Dorothy. **Costumes and Textiles of the Aztec Indians**. Los Angeles: Southwest Museum, 1940.

Davis, Mary L. and Greta Pack. **Mexican Jewelry**. Tucson: University of Texas Press, 1976.

D'Harcourt, Raoul. **Textiles of Ancient Peru**. Seattle: University of Washington Press, 1975.

Dunbarton Oaks Handbook. **Pre-Columbian Art**. Robert Woods Bliss Collection, Washington, D.C.

Enciso, Jorge. **Designs from Pre-Columbian Mexico**. New York: Dover Publications, Inc., 1971.

Mosely, Michael. **Peru's Golden Treasures**. Chicago: The Field Museum, 1978.

Rowe, Ann Pollard. **Warp-Patterned Weaves of the Andes**. Washington, D.C.: Textile Museum, 1977.

Tushingham, A.D. **Gold for the Gods**. Ontario: Royal Ontario Museum, 1976.

Vexler, Jill. **Mexican Textiles, Line and Color**. Tamayo, Mexico: Museo Ruffino, 1986.

Needleweaving

Dendel, Esther Warner. **Needleweaving: Easy as Embroidery**. Philadelphia, PA: Countryside Press, 1971.

John, Edith. **Needleweaving.** Newton, Mass: Charles T. Branford Co., 1970.

Nordfors, Jill. **Needlelace and Needleweaving: A New Look at Traditional Stitches**. Livermore, CA: Aardvark Adventures, 1985.

Howell-Koehler, Nancy. **Soft Jewelry: Design, Techniques & Materials.** Englewood Cliffs, NJ: Prentice Hall, Inc., 1977.

Magazines

Fiberarts
50 College Street
Asheville, NC 28801

Ornament
PO Box 2349
San Marcos, CA 92069
Focus: Beads, Jewelry and Wearable Art

Threads
Taunton Press
63 South Main St.
Newtown, CT 06470-5506

Bead Societies

Bead Societies

Joining a local bead society will bring you in contact with others who share your enthusiasm for beads and provide a way to learn more about beads and how to use them. Write to a bead society that is near you for more information and a sample copy of their newsletter. If your community doesn't have a bead society, you can start one!

Alaska

Juneau Bead Society
  c/o The Bead Gallery
  201 Seward
  Juneau, AK 99801

Arizona

Arizona Bead Society
  Box 80111
  Arcadia Station 072
  Phoenix, AZ 85060-0111

California

Bead Society of Los Angeles
  PO Box 241874
  Culver City, CA 90024-9674

The Northern California Bead Society
  1650 Lower Grand Ave.
  Piedmont, CA 94611

District of Columbia

Bead Society of Greater Washington
  PO Box 70036
  Chevy Chase, MD 20813-0036

Florida

Bead Society of Central Florida
  121 Larkspur Drive
  Altamonte Springs, FL 32701

Illinois

The Bead Society of Greater
  Chicago
  8420 West Bryn Mawr, Suite 600
  Chicago, IL 60631

Chicago Midwest Bead Society
  1020 Davis Street
  Evanston, IL 60201

Maryland

Baltimore Bead Society
  PO Box 311
  Riderwood, MD 21139-0311

Massachusetts

Beadesigner International
  PO Box 503
  Lincoln, MA 01173

Massachusetts Bead Soceity
  119 Burlington
  Lexington, MA 02173

Minnesota

Upper Midwest Bead Society
  c/o Beautiful Beads
  115 Hennepin Avenue
  Minneapolis, MN 55401

New Jersey

Bead Society of New Jersey
  P.O. Box 7465
  Shrewsbury, NJ 07702

New Mexico

New Mexico Bead Society
  PO Box 36824
  Albuquerque, NM 87176-6824

New York

The Bead Society of Greater New
  York
  Fashion Institute of Technology
  P.O. Box 427
  New York, NY 10116-0427

Ohio

Bead Society of Central Ohio
  C/O Byzantium
  249 King Ave.
  Columbus, OH 43201

Oregon

The Portland Bead Society
  PO Box 10611
  Portland, OR 97210

Texas

Austin Bead Society
  600 Greenhill Drive, #920
  Round Rock, TX 78664

Dallas Bead Society
  10407 Shadow Bend Drive
  Dallas, TX 75230

Virginia

Northern Virginia Bead Society
  11721 Fireside Place #E
  Reston, VA 22090

Washington

The Northwest Bead Society
5450 39th Ave West
Seattle, WA 98199

Olympic Bead Society
PO Box 27
Quilcene, WA 98376

Great Britain

Bead Society of Great Britain
c/o Carole Morris
1 Casburn Lane
Burwell, Cambridgeshire,
CB5 OED
United Kingdom

Bead Organizations

The Bead Museum
140 S. Montezuma
Prescott, AZ 86301

Center for the Study of Beadwork
PO Box 13719
Portland, OR 97213

Center for Bead Research
4 Essex St.
Lake Placid, NY 12946

The Society of Bead Researchers
6500 Romaine St. #7
Los Angeles, CA 90038

The Bead Study Trust
Talland, Fullers Road
Rowledge, Farnham
Surrey
GU10 4DF England

Supplies

Warp Thread: Three-ply waxed Irish linen thread, 18 gauge, is an ideal warp thread. It is available from Victor Kemp Upholstery Supply, 523 North Alvarado Street, Los Angeles, CA 90026, tel. 213-413-2464. It comes is several colors on 4 ounce spools. A second source of waxed linen thread is Royalwood Ltd., 517 Woodville Road, Mansfield, OH 44907, tel. 419-526-1630.

Pins: The heavy-duty pins which hold the warp in place on the board are available in office supply stores as "bank pins." They are also available from Champion Office Products, 1812 Duke St., Alexandria, VA 22314, tel. 703-836-0877.

"Watercolor Threads" are from the Caron Collection, 67 Poland Street, Bridgeport, CT 06605.

Sources of Beads

Begin by checking the Yellow Pages under beads, craft supplies or jewelry for local sources and check Ornament Magazine advertisers for mail order companies.

Photo and Illustration Credits

Cover Photos

Subject:	Photographer
Necklace: Song of India #2	Richard Rodriguez
End Papers	Richard Rodriguez

Chapter One

No.	Name	Artist	Photographer
1.	Le Grande Kabyle	Helen Banes	Joel Breger
2.	Diane Fitzgerald		Corry Skaarnes
3.	Helen Banes		Richard Rodriguez
4.	Spirit Lock of Thailand.	Helen Banes	Richard Rodriguez
5.	Homage to Maria Martinez	Helen Banes	Joel Breger
6.	Timbuktu	Helen Banes	Richard Rodriguez
7.	Fetish Adornment	Helen Banes	Joel Breger
8.	Asante Gold	Helen Banes	Joel Breger
9.	Tairona Pectoral	Helen Banes	Richard Rodriguez
10.	Peruvian Pectoral with Coins	Helen Banes	Richard Rodriguez
11.	Tolima Figure	Helen Banes	William L. Allen
12.	Mask of Xipe-Totec	Helen Banes	Richard Rodriguez
13.	Mask of Xipe-Totec (Detail)	Helen Banes	Richard Rodriguez
14.	Brazilian Tribal	Helen Banes	William L. Allen
15.	Colombian Gold	Helen Banes	Joel Breger
16.	Royal Pectoral with Scarab	Helen Banes	Joel Breger
17.	Chinese Cloud Collar	Helen Banes	Joel Breger
18.	Clarisse's Collar	Helen Banes	Richard Rodriguez
19.	Coral Cascade	Helen Banes	Joel Breger
20.	Tiffany No. 2	Helen Banes	Richard Rodriguez
21.	Urim and Thummim.	Helen Banes	Richard Rodriguez
22.	Scarab	Judy Benson	Judy Benson
23.	Frog	Judy Benson	Judy Benson
24.	Lady Helen	Christofer Aven	Christofer Aven
25.	First Effort	Judy Ehrhardt	Jim Caulfield
26.	Aztec Night	Judy Ehrhardt	Jim Caulfield
27.	Autumn Blaze	Kimberly Childs	Kimberly Childs
28.	Nantucket Fantasy	Virginia E. Hird	James V. Dorn
29.	Andean Starburst	Virginia E. Hird	James V. Dorn
30.	Orpheum	Barbara Hjort	Barbara Hjort
31.	Seventeen Blue	Barbara Hjort	Barbara Hjort
32.	Jeweltone	Barbara Hjort	Barbara Hjort
33.	Geode	Barbara Hjort	Diane Fitzgerald
34.	Sun Dance	Pamela Penney	Pamela Penney
35.	Flora	Pamela Penney	Pamela Penney
36.	Victorian Parlor	Patricia Jeydel	James Dain
37.	Inca Princess	Diane Fitzgerald	Diane Fitzgerald
38.	Of Royal Blood	Diane Fitzgerald	Diane Fitzgerald
39.	Miss Piggy	Diane Fitzgerald	Diane Fitzgerald
40.	Anasazi Bird	Ann Shafer	Edward Taylor
41.	Untitled No. 1	Barbara Saslow	Roberta F. Raeburn
42.	Untitled No. 2	Barbara Saslow	Roberta F. Raeburn
43.	Untitled	Jadine Surette	Martin P. Amt
44.	Sacred Nymph	Kathleen B. Williams	Ronnie Haber
45.	Sea Fantasy	Deborah Tweedy	Deborah Tweedy
46.	Egyptian Geometry	Diane Fitzgerald	Diane Fitzgerald
47.	Untitled	Diane Fitzgerald	Diane Fitzgerald
48.	Monkey Tree	Diane Fitzgerald	Diane Fitzgerald
49.	Sun, Steps and Shadows	Daniele Du Bois	Martin P. Amt
50.	**Africa II**	**Carroll Gotte**	Martin P. Amt
51.	A God's Promise	Phyllis Magrab	Martin P. Amt
52.	Pre-Columbian I	Carroll Gotte	Martin P. Amt

53.	Bedouin II	Carroll Gotte	Martin P. Amt
54.	Pre-Columbian II	Carroll Gotte	Martin P. Amt
55.	Waterfall	Sarah Johnson	Martin P. Amt
56.	Diver's World	Sarah Johnson	Martin P. Amt
57.	Lepidoptera	Frances L. Eyster	Martin P. Amt
58.	Asian Fantasy	Ilene Shefferman	Martin P. Amt
59.	All That Jazz	Ilene Shefferman	Martin P. Amt
60.	Ganges	Gretchen Prewitt	Martin P. Amt
61.	Tapestry Necklace	Joan Wack	Martin P. Amt
62.	Inca Kilim	Rebecca Toner	Martin P. Amt
63.	Summer's Joy	Joyce Collin-Bushell	David T. Bushell
64.	Untitled No. 1	Virginia Hudak	Martin P. Amt
65.	Untitled No. 3	Virginia Hudak	Martin P. Amt
66.	Twenties Angles	Eugenia Nowlin	Martin P. Amt
67.	Song of India	Eugenia Nowlin	Martin P. Amt
68.	Fertility	Sheila Miller	Martin P. Amt
69.	African Adornment	Eurla Frederick	Martin P. Amt
70.	The Egyptian Way	Eurla Frederick	Martin P. Amt
71.	A Puppet Show	Eurla Frederick	Martin P. Amt
72.	Falling Leaves	M. A. Klein	M. A. Klein
73.	Moonlit Night	M. A. Klein	M. A. Klein
74.	Untitled	Rose Madri	Sepp Seitz
75.	Untitled	Pat Norman	Pat Norman

Students' Pre-Columbian Interpretation

76.	Moche, Turquoise and Gold	Sheila Miller	Martin P. Amt
77.	Tumi	Sheila Miller	Martin P. Amt
78.	Untitled	Frances Eyster	Martin P. Amt
79.	Royal Arsenal	Gretchen Prewitt	Martin P. Amt
80.	Untitled	Jimmylene Wertman	Martin P. Amt
81.	Untitled No. 2	Jimmylene Wertman	Martin P. Amt
82.	Mayan Mask	Ileen Shefferman	Martin P. Amt
83.	Untitled	Phyllis Baez	Martin P. Amt
84.	Untitled	Phyllis Magrab	Martin P. Amt
85.	Cam's Frog	Marion Boyer	Martin P. Amt
86.	Figuratively Feline	Cookie Labby	Martin P. Amt
87.	Untitled	Daniele DuBois	Martin P. Amt
88.	Noble Warrior	Eugenia Nowlin	Martin P. Amt
89.	Flying Frog Pectoral	Edward Hyland	Martin P. Amt
90.	Nazca Huari Pectoral	Joanne Bast	Martin P. Amt
91.	Falling Girl with Cat	Bonnie Dunn	Martin P. Amt
92.	Bird Pin	Maggie Wheeler	Maggie Wheeler

Chapter Two

No.	Photographer
93.	Martin P. Amt
94.	Martin P. Amt
95.	Joel Breger
96.	Joel Breger
97.	Richard Rodriguez

Chapter Two - Figures

Ancient Egyptian Motifs and Ancient Chinese Motifs by James Kiehne

Other illustrations by Diane Fitzgerald

Chapter Three

No.	Photographer
98. to 112.	Diane Fitzgerald
113.	Joel Breger
114.	Diane Fitzgerald
115.	Diane Fitzgerald
116.	Joel Breger
117. to 120.	Susan Ramseier Paepcke
121.	Martin P. Amt

Figures

No	Subject	Illustrator
17.	Pin Placement	Diane Fitzgerald
18.	Slip Knot	James Kiehne
19.	Neckline Edge	Diane Fitzgerald
20.	Warping Diagram	Diane Fitzgerald
21.	Sales Tag Knot	James Kiehne
22.	Weaving Diagram	Diane Fitzgerald
23.	4-Strand Braid	Sue Roche

Chapter Four

No	Photographer
122.	L. Barnaby
123.	Diane Fitzgerald
124.	Diane Fitzgerald
125.	William L. Allen
126.	Diane Fitzgerald
127.	Richard Rodriguez
128.	Diane Fitzgerald
129.	Diane Fitzgerald
130.	William L. Allen
131.	Richard Rodriguez
132.	Martin P. Amt
133.	Richard Rodriguez
134.	Martin P. Amt
135.	Diane Fitzgerald
136.	Martin P. Amt
137.	William L. Allen
138.	Joel Breger
139.	Joel Breger
140.	William L. Allen
141.	William L. Allen
142.	William L. Allen

Chapter Five

Figures

24.	Paper Bead Shapes	Diane Fitzgerald

Photos

143.	Diane Fitzgerald
144.	Diane Fitzgerald
145.	Penny Diamanti
146.	Joel Breger
147.	Joel Breger
148.	Joel Breger
149.	Helen Banes
150.	Richard Rodriguez
151.	Penny Diamanti
152.	Penny Diamanti
153.	Martin P. Amt
154.	Joel Breger

Index

African Inspired - 84
Amber - 116
Amulets - 116
Art Deco Motifs - 50
Art Deco Style - 51, 76, 131
Art Nouveau Necklace - 124
Balance - 33, 41
Bead Bazaar - 115
Bead Threader - 57
Beads - 60
    Adding - 60
    Adventurine - 117
    Coral - 117
    Crystal - 118
    Displaying - 118
    Dough - 120
    Grouping -
    Jet - 117
    Lamp - 116
    Paper - 119
    Polymer Clay - 121
    Storing - 118
    Stringing on Warp - 61
    Wire - 120
    Wood - 117
    Wrapped - 120
Beater - 57
Braid, Four Strand - 67
Chinese Symbol - 45
Chinese Motifs - 45
Closures, Adjustable - 69
Color: Bridges - 34
    Changing - 63, 65
    Schemes - 35
    Wheel - 34

Colors:
    Analogous - 35
    Complementary - 35
Crimps - 62
Crochet Hook - 60
Diagonal Color Changes - 63
Dovetailing - 63
Egyptian Motifs - 44
Eye of Horus - 44
Finishing Techniques - 55, 66
Fetish Necklace - 121
Focal Point - 33, 40
Fray Prevention - 57
Gem and Mineral Dealers - 114
Geometric Pattern - 100
Graph Paper - 55
Headpins - 56
Interlocking Weave - 63
Jewelry, Fish & Coin - 63
Knots, Lark's Head - 62
    Sales Tag - 62
Line - 33, 37
Monochromatic - 35
Monofilament Line - 60
Navajo Inspired - 94
Neckedge - 58
Needles - 56
North American Motifs - 48
Ojime - 114
Oriental Motif - 88
Patterns - 73
Perle Cotton - 56
Pin Placement - 57
Plain Weave - 63
Pre-Columbian Motifs - 49

Rhythm - 33, 42
Scale - 33, 41
Scarab - 121, 122
Shades - 34
Shape - 33, 39, 64
Slip Knot - 58
Slits, Weaving - 63, 64, 69
Supplies - 55
Supports & Closures - 66, 68
    Adjustable - 69
    Beaded Woven Support - 67
    Woven Support - 69
    Wrapped Support - 69
Symbolism - 33, 43
Symbols -
    Art Deco - 50
    Chinese - 45
    Egyptian - 44
    North American - 48
    Pre-Columbian - 49
Talismans - 116
Texture - 33, 40
Thread, Adding New - 65
Tints - 34
Tools - 53
Value - 35
Warp - 55, 57, 59
Warp Stringing - 57
Warp Endings - 57
Weaving: a Shape - 64
            a Slit - 63
Weft - 59
Working Board - 57